ADEWALE MAJA-PEARCE was born in London in 1953.
He grew up in Lagos, Nigeria, but returned to London to
complete his education and gained a Master of Arts degree in
African Studies at the School of Oriental and African Studies.
He has held various positions in the literary world, is presently
Africa Editor of the journal *Index on Censorship*, and also Series
Editor of the African Writers Series.

His literary achievements include a collection of short
stories about Nigeria, *Loyalties and Other Stories* (Longman,
1987); a travelogue, *In My Father's Country* (William
Heinemann, 1987); and the scholarly poetry anthology, *Okigbo:
Collected Poems* (Heinemann, 1986) which Maja-Pearce edited.
His most recent work is *How Many Miles to Babylon?* (William
Heinemann, 1990).

I have one abiding religion: human liberty

WOLE SOYINKA

ADEWALE MAJA-PEARCE

WHO'S AFRAID OF WOLE SOYINKA?

Essays On Censorship

Heinemann International Literature and Textbooks
a division of Heinemann Educational Books Ltd
Halley Court, Jordan Hill, Oxford OX2 8EJ

Heinemann Educational Books Inc
361 Hanover Street, Portsmouth, New Hampshire, 03801, USA

Heinemann Educational Books (Nigeria) Ltd
PMB 5205, Ibadan
Heinemann Kenya Ltd
Kijabe Street, PO Box 45314, Nairobi
Heinemann Educational Boleswa
PO Box 10103, Village Post Office, Gaborone, Botswana

LONDON   EDINBURGH   PARIS   MADRID
ATHENS   BOLOGNA   MELBOURNE
SYDNEY   AUCKLAND   SINGAPORE
TOKYO   HARARE

British Library Cataloguing in Publication Data
Maja-Pearce, Adewale
Who's afraid of Wole Soyinka?: essays on censorship.
1. Censorship
I. Title
363.31
ISBN 0–435–90977–0

Acknowledgements
The publishers would like to thank the following for their permission to use copyright
material: Marie Claire and World Press Network Ltd for 'Lagos: A City Under Siege',
cited in this book as 'Fear and Loathing in Lagos', Copyright © UK Marie Claire/WPN.
The publishers have made every effort to chase copyright holders but we would be very
glad to hear from any one who has been inadvertently overlooked and make the necessary
changes at the first opportunity

Phototypeset by Wilmaset, Birkenhead, Wirral
Printed in England by Clays Ltd, St Ives plc

91 92 93 94 10 9 8 7 6 5 4 3 2 1

Contents

To the memory of George Theiner,
1927–1988

Introduction

The bulk of these essays first appeared in *Index on Censorship* magazine, where I work as the Africa editor. One of the few exceptions is 'Fear and Loathing in Lagos', which was commissioned by a London-based women's magazine and which, therefore, concerned itself with the position of women in Nigerian society. My argument in the essay was that the inferior status accorded women reflected the continuing stranglehold of feudal relationships, and that this went a long way to explain the failure of the society to enter into a modern relationship with the century. Straightforward enough, one would have thought, and hardly controversial: I didn't even allude to the widespread practice of child marriage (or, more accurately, rape) where ten-year-old girls are turned into breeding machines with the inevitable tragic results. However, it wasn't long before the question of censorship reared its head even in this regard when certain sections of the Nigerian community, always ready to defend to the death the honour of their country (to say nothing of 'their' women), took me to task for conveying what they were pleased to call a 'negative' image of the country in a foreign publication. It seems that my essay not only displayed a deplorable lack of patriotism but, worse, gave succour to Nigeria's enemies at the same time as it turned me into a modern-day Judas: 'It would have been different if *marie claire* was not paying you for your mis-directed social concern,' one of them wrote; 'I see it as the moral equivalent of blood money.'

My rejoinder, reproduced here as a postscript to the essay, is already in danger of taking these self-styled patriots more seriously than they deserve. In any case, what they said was less interesting than the language they used to say it; specifically, the level of hysteria they betrayed ('the moral equivalent of blood money'), and the way that hysteria sought to avoid any direct engagement with an argument they didn't want to hear. So much the worse for them: as I write, a recently-formed Women's Centre in Nigeria is soliciting for funds to combat 'violence against women, including assault, genital mutilation, rape, battery, murder, infanticide and cruel neglect', which they identify as 'the least recognised human rights issue in the world'. The fact that their appeal appeared in the pages of the 'Western' media might mean that the organisers are themselves guilty of a lack of patriotism; if so, then it is the definition of patriotism which is at fault.

And what is true of Nigeria is equally true of the continent as a whole, but to put the blame for Africa's present predicament – hunger, disease, wars and rumours of wars – only on the excesses of brutal governments is to misunderstand the scale of the problem. To be sure, the continent can boast a legion of tyrants the equal of any, beginning with President-for-Life Dr Hastings Kamuzu Banda of Malawi ('I will keep them there and they will rot. And I am going to make sure that in addition to the regular prison officers we have additional warders who will know what to do with these fools'); but the distance between the dictators who murder poets and the men who rape girls must be measured, after all, by the absence of justice in either case. 'Do we have courts in Nigeria?' was the question recently posed by Fela Anikulapo-Kuti, the musician. Indeed: during my first visit to Liberia in 1988, as part of the journey which formed the title essay of this collection, I met a journalist who was beaten with a fan belt every day for six months for suggesting that President Doe had lost the elections. He was never charged with any crime, much less brought to trial.

Always, in Africa, it is the individual who must risk everything for an idea of what their societies could be, but this is inescapable in societies where the institutions of the modern democratic state are deliberately subverted by reactionaries who, lacking a larger idea of human relations, wish only to perpetuate themselves and their kind in power. The fact that a few brave souls are prepared to go the distance is, of course, the continent's only hope of salvation; but why the brightest and the best should be forced to sacrifice themselves in this way is a question that wouldn't even be recognised for what it was by the cacophonous parade of mediocrities who are pleased to call themselves . . . patriots. And how could they, lacking even the language with which to ask it? The story of post-colonial Africa is the story of failure at every level, but to close your ears and raise your voice in order to deny this is hardly an adequate response.

'The time has come to stop apologising for our mistakes,' a Nigerian friend, a poet, said to me recently. 'We have to take a hard look at ourselves and be prepared to write the truth, however painful.' The tone of these essays, in the tradition of the essay itself, is deliberately combative. For this reason, they appear here as they were first published, even those which express views I might now be inclined to modify. This is especially true of the essays on South Africa, where I argue that the fact of apartheid makes that country unique on the continent. But this is an over-simplification. Apartheid operates in one form or another throughout Africa – and not only as regards women – which is why students at a Nigerian university refused to celebrate the release of Nelson Mandela on the irrefutable grounds that there were any number of Mandelas currently incarcerated in Nigerian prisons. They also pointed out that it was inconceivable for a person to spend twenty-seven years in a Nigerian cell and still be able to walk out, as anyone who has read the recent report by the Civil Liberties Organisation (CLO) will discover.

But at least the CLO is able to function in Nigeria. Such an organisation couldn't exist in almost any other country on the continent, as was recently proved when a similar group of young lawyers in Kenya, attempting to copy the Nigerian example, were simply taken into custody and held without charge or trial. Unfortunately, they had made the mistake of taking seriously the noises they were beginning to hear from Western governments that future aid will be determined by the relevant country's human rights record. It is difficult, given Western governments' own record vis-a-vis Africa, to take such noises seriously; and one is at least sympathetic to the view expressed by the former President of Chad who was moved to dismiss such talk as merely 'this year's fashion in Paris'. As regards Kenya, we know that it was the British government which ensured President Moi's accession to power following the death of Kenyatta, just as we know the extent of British investment in the country as reward for its perceived 'stability'.

In the end, of course, Africa's salvation lies in Africa itself, which is why the obsession with what the West thinks is not only wrong-headed but, in its slavish dependence on the other person's good opinion, is itself part of the continent's continuing tragedy. Which is also why these essays attempt, as Wole Soyinka once put it, to look inwards, into the present, 'into the obvious symptoms of the niggling, warning, predictable present, from which alone (lies) the salvation of ideals'.

1990

THE
ESSAYS

Who's afraid of Wole Soyinka?

1

'But no', Mr Nelson said, turning his yellow malicious eyes
over the pointed leaking huts, 'we don't like Faulkner.' After a
while he found enough vitality to explain. 'You see, he has an
idea.'

'What idea?' I said.

'Nobody knows,' Mr Nelson said, 'but we don't like it.'

Graham Greene: *Journey Without Maps*

It didn't take me long to find Kabral. As a former director of the
Institute of Journalism in Accra, he was well-known within
newspaper circles. When I arrived at his office, a bare room with
two wooden tables and an assortment of broken-down chairs, he
was putting the final touches to the weekly sports paper he
currently edits with Kweku Baako. In the present so-called
'culture of silence', which has become the dominant feature of
life in Ghana since Flt. Lt. Jerry John Rawlings – 'Junior Jesus' to
his many admirers – assumed power for the second time five and
a half years ago, these four-page sports weeklies are the only
outlet for the country's self-respecting journalists. I counted
fifteen of them; someone told me there were at least twenty. By
all accounts Ghanaians are football-mad, but for a country with a
population of only twelve million this number seemed rather
excessive.

I had first met Kabral in London the previous year, where he had come to do a one-year course at the London School of Economics as a respite from the hazards of journalism in a country which, under the leadership of Kwame Nkrumah in the late fifties and early sixties, had once been the showcase of Africa. The paper he had then edited, the *Free Press*, was forced to close down following official harrassment and what Kabral identified, in an article he wrote for us while he was in London (Ghana's *Free Press*, *Index* 1/87), as lack of support from the public they were ostensibly serving:

> What has kept us going is a realisation that what we write is but an echo of secret murmuring and complaints of the wider society. But in a society where everyone feels so emasculated as to only complain in the secrecy of their bedrooms, a time comes when lonely voices feel the compulsion to behave like all the others.

Indeed, Kabral's predecessor in the editor's chair, John Kugblenu, died a few weeks after he was released from detention, presumably from wounds inflicted under interrogation at the notorious Nsawam Medium Prison.

Later, over lunch at an open-air restaurant, Kweku Baako, the former research assistant with the *Free Press*, alluded to his own experience in detention. A small, soft-spoken man, I had to lean forward to catch his words:

'Altogether I was inside for more than a year without charge or trial. They kept coming day and night. Different people. By the end of the second week I was lying on the floor of my cell covered in my own shit and piss. A doctor came. He said: "If this man doesn't receive immediate medical attention he will be dead within a week."

'That doctor saved my life. If not for him I wouldn't be here today. Afterwards it wasn't so bad except they wouldn't allow anybody to visit me, not even my family. My mother was looking for me everywhere. She didn't know where I was, or even if I was still alive.'

Who's afraid of Wole Soyinka?

At that moment, as if on cue, a soldier entered. Kweku fell silent and watched him cross the courtyard. I thought, at first, that he was understandably fearful of being overheard, part of that culture of silence which made people instinctively lower their voices and glance over their shoulders whenever the topic of conversation became politically sensitive; but I was soon to understand, as I got to know him a little better, that a man who has been so close to death can no longer be easily intimidated. In a sense, the worst had been done to him. And when the soldier, a major, disappeared into an adjoining room, Kweku leaned forward and said:

'That was my first interrogator. He knows me but he won't look at me. We grew up together in this very district, about two streets away. I see him from time to time but he never looks at me.'

A moment later the major re-emerged and walked briskly back the way he had come, eyes fixed in front, his dark glasses giving nothing away. Kweku, as before, watched him come to within a foot of our table. It wasn't possible to read Kweku's expression, and my imagination couldn't encompass the conflicting thoughts that must have been stirred up by so unwelcome a sight. Perhaps his silence was his only weapon; perhaps it was the only kind of revenge possible, always assuming that revenge is among the human possibilities. I don't know. I only know that I felt an impersonal hatred for the uniformed thug, and not merely because I had been drawn to Kweku from the first, by what I recognised as an unusual kind of courage and integrity.

I had seen that integrity in Kabral, and I was to see it again and again in more than a few of the journalists I encountered during my trip through four countries, from Nigeria to Sierra Leone. In Liberia, for instance, I was fortunate to track down Rufus Darpoh because the newspaper he edited, the *Sun Times*, had been closed down for allegedly publishing articles considered 'hostile' to the government and thereby 'creating tension and instability'. This was not his first brush with the authorities, and even he had lost count of the number of times his paper had been

3

summarily closed for offending the powers-that-be. He was now working in an advisory capacity for a paper sponsored by the Catholic Church in order to bring in a little money until he was allowed to resume publication. And yet – who could blame him? – he wasn't sure that he wanted the hassles any longer. He was weary of the constant harassment, the sudden invitation in the middle of the night to visit the Executive Mansion.

'The last time I went President Doe said: "You journalists are careless with your lives." How was I supposed to respond? He kept me there for three hours. During that time he told me that he himself was invincible, that even if somebody came into the room right then and opened fire with a machine gun he wouldn't be killed. He said that some people were trying to harm him with *juju* but they wouldn't succeed.'

It didn't occur to me to doubt what he said. President Samuel Kenyon Doe, a thirty-five-year-old former Master-Sergeant and now (courtesy of the South Koreans) a doctor of philosophy, is reported to be mentally unstable. Rumours abound of cannibalism in the Executive Mansion, a practice which had featured in an article on the abortive coup in 1985, 'How Quiwonkpa and Gbenyon died', which appeared in *West Africa* magazine (23/30 December 1985):

> At the Barclay Training Ground, before hundreds of spectators, Quiwonkpa's body was chopped up into bits in a macabre cannibalistic ritual by some of Doe's soldiers who, astonishingly in these modern times, still believe that by eating bits of a great warrior's body, some of that greatness would come to them. The heart, of course, was the prize delicacy and it is traditionally shared on a hierarchical basis. The blood-curdling dismemberment of Quiwonkpa was carried out in the open before hundreds of market women and shoppers who had trooped in from the Rally Time market to see if indeed Quiwonkpa had been killed. I personally saw two soldiers outside the 'Talk of the Town' pub on Macdonald Street dangling what they said was Quiwonkpa's manhood. Other

media colleagues reported seeing two fingers, presumably Quiwonkpa's, at Water Street, being dangled by jubilant soldiers who indicated they would devour their prize trophy at the end of the day.

This fitted in with a report I had read while preparing for my trip. *Liberia: A Promise Betrayed*, published in 1986 by the US-based Lawyers Committee for Human Rights, portrayed a society held together by the use of naked terror perpetrated on the citizens by a whole panoply of security agencies, including the 'elite' Israeli-trained Special Anti-Terrorist Unit. A particularly horrific case study concerned the attack on the country's only university in 1984 when, in response to a peaceful demonstration, a detachment of two hundred soldiers killed 'an undetermined number' of students in the course of an operation that lasted five days. The university was subsequently closed and a number of lecturers fled overseas, proving once again that dictatorships are notoriously wasteful of their assets.

I caught a glimpse of the way the security forces operate the day I crossed the border from Cote d'Ivoire and was confronted with the words I was to hear over and over again until I quit the country four days later: 'What have you got for me?'; although in all fairness I ought to add that this phrase, in one variation or another, was not unique to Liberia. Africa is graft and corruption all the way. I mean this in an absolute sense. At the end of my trip, for instance, as I waited for my flight at the airport in Sierra Leone, I sat next to an Englishman who was busy dispensing crisp twenty Leone notes (twenty-five pence at black market rates) to everyone who came up to him – customs, immigration, police, security, somebody 'in diamonds'. He was obviously what they call an old Africa hand, and he certainly knew the score. It was all so matter-of-fact, so normal: he didn't even glance at some of the recipients of his largesse, simply passed them the money as he carried on his conversation.

One of the hazards of travelling by road was to be confronted at regular intervals by officials of one sort or another demanding their 'dash' before we were permitted to proceed. The only difference lay in the style of the particular country in which I happened to be. In Ghana, it was a soldier standing in the rain at three o'clock in the morning begging for one hundred cedis (twenty pence); in Cote d'Ivoire, more prosperous and self-assured, it was necessary for each of us on the coach to give money to the driver to distribute along the way. But in Liberia, without niceties of any sort, these demands took on a more sinister edge, or so I imagined, by the hand-me-down New York police uniforms, the incongruous American accent, and the inevitable dark glasses. The cumulative effect was like some-body's perverted idea of a Hollywood B-movie, the more so as the actors themselves obviously took their role very seriously indeed. It might have helped if they were able to see the absurdity of their appearance, but self-knowledge is not among the attributes of hired thugs.

'What is your profession?'

'I work for a publisher.'

'Publisher?'

'Yes, book publisher.'

My answers, purposely brief – never volunteer more than you have to, but always keep as close to the truth as possible – were written slowly and with considerable effort. These officials, I soon discovered, were semi-literate, like the President himself who, by his own admission, didn't see the inside of a school until he was fifteen.

'What is your business in Liberia?'

'I'm just visiting.'

'*Visiting!*' The disbelief was genuine and told me everything I needed to know about the country's image of itself. Perhaps it is this that makes possible a certain kind of barbarity, a cheapening of life in a dependent country that produces nothing but a distorted reflection of a foreign power: Liberia, settled by freed American slaves who dominated the politics of the country from 1847 until their overthrow in 1980, visited upon the natives the plantation conditions they had left behind. So much so, in fact,

6

that as late as 1930 a League of Nations International Commission of Inquiry revealed the widespread existence of slavery within the country.

It is humiliating to discover just how swiftly another human being can generate fear in you and make you behave in ways which you loathe in yourself even as you smile ingratiatingly. There I was on an empty road with night falling – abruptly, as it does in the tropics; light one minute, darkness the next – and I found myself, faced with a man for whom my life was of absolutely no account, involuntarily wanting to please him but understanding at the same time the baseness of what I was doing. I despised the man and what he stood for, but he had power and I didn't. How far might I be forced to go in order to preserve my life, which suddenly seemed fragile and for that reason precious? I don't know, but I was only too conscious of what it meant to be a practising journalist in such a country, at least one who maintained an idea of the journalist's proper function. Rufus could simply have buckled – or left town.

Leaving town was always a possibility. Kabral said: 'People were surprised to see me back in Accra when I finished my course in London. They thought I had gone for good. But this is my country; where else am I supposed to go?' And yet, I didn't imagine that his present occupation gave him much satisfaction. I was right. He said: 'I'm not a sports journalist but I can't work for any of the so-called newspapers. At least with football I can write the truth. I do the best I can; I try to be professional. I'm not ashamed of what I'm doing.'

I was to understand what he meant when he took me round to see the staff on the largest-circulation newspaper, the *People's Daily Graphic*. The figure of one hundred and fifty thousand in daily sales was quoted by everyone I met, but later, as we walked back to the car, we were confronted by a telling sight: all over the courtyard of the extensive premises, and all along the outside wall between the building and the main road, great piles of unsold newspapers dating back a month were being bought in job-lots by women traders who would use them to wrap the food they sold in

7

the market. Considering the contents of the paper it was perhaps a fitting end to what can only be described as the government's willing mouthpiece: the visit of a government minister to some wretched village to harangue the peasants on the necessity of growing more food was that day's lead story, followed by a badly-written account of the latest efforts by the authorities to stop cross-border cattle smuggling. Kabral watched me take it all in, then he smiled and said: 'You believe what they told you?'

The pity of it is that the *Daily Graphic*, up until two years ago, was still considered the best paper in the country, though even then people were beginning to complain that its coverage of national affairs was insufficiently critical of the Rawlings regime. Their suspicions were confirmed when, in early 1986, an editorial appeared in support of a government order banning workers' leave allowances. The order was later rescinded after widespread industrial action, and then it was discovered that the editorial had in fact been written by an official in the Castle Information Bureau (CIB). The CIB is the government's main propaganda organ. Its office is in Osu Castle, the seat of government. It is headed, incongruously enough, by an elderly Englishwoman, Valerie Sackey. She was pointed out to me one day as she was being driven around central Accra in an official Land Rover. With her pale skin and her thinning white hair she wouldn't have looked out of place in an English county town.

A subsequent meeting of the staff of the *Daily Graphic* passed a vote of no confidence against the government-appointed editor. Predictably enough, the authorities resisted demands that he be removed. Such editors, and the journalists who have elected to continue working under them, are perhaps better described as state-appointed bureaucrats whose task is not so much to report the news as to re-cycle bulletins handed down to them from the lofty heights of the CIB, like so many civil servants faithfully carrying out government directives.

Government control of the media is especially evident in the work of the Ghana News Agency (GNA), Independent Africa's first news agency founded by Nkrumah in 1958 to ensure that the continent's voice would be heard in world affairs. Nkrumah, whatever his later excesses, was an astute politician with a genuine vision. He understood that Africa would continue to be misrepresented for as long as it was dependent on foreign perceptions. The GNA was one of a number of institutions, like the Institute for African Studies at the University of Ghana, which was set up to correct the historical imbalance. If a building alone is enough to change history then the GNA would now be competing on equal terms with Reuters and Tass and Agence France Presse, but an undertaking of this magnitude depends on more than just the outward symbols, as the current Soviet leadership has discovered. Reporters must be able to report. As the GNA presently operates, all copy sent in from around the country is channelled through the office in Accra where it is vetted before it is passed on to the local papers. The head of the GNA is a government appointee who knows what is acceptable to his political masters.

The same treatment is given to reports from the outside agencies, to which, in any case, and with the exception of the American-owned Associated Press, only the GNA is permitted to subscribe. Some of the 'editing' is ludicrous, and one wonders why they bother. For example, any reference to fellow Socialist countries, such as Zimbabwe and Ethiopia, must always be positive; the government of South Africa is always 'racist'. As regards the latter, the idea seemed to be that Ghanaian journalists might be in some doubt as to the particular evils of apartheid, and so must be alerted at every opportunity. The end result is the debasement of language, as it always is in authoritarian states: if every reference to South Africa is prefixed by 'racist', then the word itself becomes meaningless.

The conclusion to be drawn from all this is that individual Ghanaians, but most especially the intellectuals, can't be trusted to interpret events in the 'correct' light, whether in their own country or abroad. This becomes sinister when you realise that the State has effectively determined that it alone has a monopoly on patriotism, and that anybody who challenges whatever interpretation it chooses to give events is a traitor. Literally so, as I was to discover. And once this principle has been established sufficiently in the collective mind the State then assumes the moral right, not to say the moral duty, to incarcerate those who disagree with them. The truth, of course, is quite the reverse. It is the imprisoned journalists who are the real patriots. One only has to listen to people like Kabral and Kweku and Rufus to see how much they love their country, and how pained they are at what is happening.

It is not surprising, then, that domestic and foreign coverage in the Ghanaian media is not only outdated but appallingly inaccurate. During the week I spent there I was reading about events which had occurred at least five days before, and then at a double-remove. As a result, nobody believes what they are told, which is why censorship is always self-defeating. Everywhere I went, and not only in Ghana but in Liberia and Sierra Leone as well, people tuned in to the BBC or the Voice of America to learn about the latest developments in their own country. So much for Nkrumah's vision: thirty years after decolonisation, Ghana continues to remain an outpost of Empire, a dependent colony with only the appearance of Independence.

As yet, the curious thing about censorship in Ghana was that it didn't appear to be *for* any specific end. The authorities had a hazy notion of what they were *against* – American imperialism, say, or Western multi-nationals – but it remained only at the level of rhetoric. This was especially ironic since the government had only recently invited the International Monetary Fund, that most capitalist of all institutions, to help solve the growing economic crisis: one needed a paper bag to carry the equivalent of fifty pounds sterling, and this in a country which, at the time of Independence in 1957, had such a surplus of foreign exchange that it had even begun to build a nuclear reactor. It was as if the overthrow of Nkrumah by the military in 1966 left a vacuum in the intellectual life of the society that could only be filled by an increasing authoritarianism, which was itself a substitute for genuine thought.

Who's afraid of Wole Soyinka?

In this Ghana was not unique. It was disturbing to find the same pattern repeated in Liberia, and again in Sierra Leone, where I stayed with the poet, Syl Cheney-Coker, who had only recently returned home after a five-year teaching stint in a Nigerian university. He currently publishes the country's only decent newspaper, *The Vanguard*, and I was privileged enough, while I was there, to watch the paper go through its fortnightly production. I ought to add that there is no daily newspaper in Sierra Leone, a melancholy fact for a country which once referred to its capital, Freetown, as 'the Athens of West Africa'.

If I say that *The Vanguard* was a labour of love I mean that Cheney-Coker lost heavily on every issue. It took three days to produce a mere two thousand copies, the maximum he could manage, even though he could easily have sold three or four times that number. Every stage of production was a major headache. The paper on which it was printed was begged from a friend in the French Embassy; the plates were set in the Government printing department through the good offices of an old classmate; the printing was done as a favour by an acquaintance who could earn twice as much by sticking to more commercial jobs: invitation cards for the Indian Association; wedding cards for the Lebanese community; calling cards for budding businessmen. This is to say nothing about the constant power failures which, for one frustrating afternoon, stopped the presses rolling for three hours. By the end of it, as we scrutinised the finished product over a beer, I hope that I managed to communicate my admiration for his guts and determination. He said: 'At some future date, when things finally get impossible and I'm forced to fold, I want it to be said that at least one person tried to produce a worthwhile newspaper.' In the meantime, he wasn't going to give up without a fight. In his regular column, 'Editor's notebook', he had written:

Many years ago, I gave up on this country. I turned my back on its needless trivialities that were becoming fashionable among the generation now in power. Without realising it we had preceded by a few years the age of the Yuppies. We measured everything by the primacy of wealth, business connections and positions. Ideas went out of the window like discarded baggage. We were in a hurry to join the age of moral bankruptcy.

Indeed; and much the same was said by Tommy Thompson, publisher of the *Free Press* until its voluntary closure, who was generous enough to take time off from a busy schedule and grant me an interview when Kabral and I turned up unannounced at his house early one evening. 'Our journalists are partly to blame. They aren't prepared to take risks. When I first started out, in the colonial days, we were ready to go to prison for what we believed in. That is what it means to be a journalist. The Nigerians understand this. They say what they feel and they accept the consequences. Here we just have small boys who only want to make money and become known in society. They don't care about what is happening around them.'

These were not idle words. Even as late as 1985 he was twice imprisoned, without charge or trial, for the support he gave his staff. Now, at sixty, he's tired. 'I've got maybe twenty years if I'm lucky,' he said. 'My wife has suffered enough and my children need me more than ever. I leave it to you people to carry on.'

But this couldn't be the whole story. It was too easy to say that the present crisis was merely a matter of chance or bad luck. Journalists could only be a barometer of a society's failings; and to the extent that Thompson had identified a crisis it was one which was perfectly understandable in terms of Africa's recent history, that same history with which Nkrumah had attempted to grapple.

It was no mistake that Tommy Thompson looked back on the colonial period as a sort of Golden Age of Ghanaian journalism, or that one looks back on Nkrumah as the only Ghanaian leader with a vision. The nature of the colonial struggle, the dream of an independent Africa free from foreign domination, acted as a unifying force across the continent. It galvanised all sections of society and gave purpose to those actively engaged in ridding the continent of European rule. Every self-respecting journalist expected to go to prison for their beliefs. But the struggle against colonialism, which absorbed all their energies, was, in intellectual terms at least, a purely negative affair masked only by what appeared to be positive results. It was also reactionary in the strict sense: it was a reaction against somebody else's ideas of how the world worked, and it drew from the very tradition against which it fought, from the ideas of Marx, Engels and Lenin which were imbibed, of all ironies, in the very heart of Empire. It was from London, after all, that Nkrumah launched his campaign.

With independence achieved the essential hollowness of the anti-colonial rhetoric resulted in an intellectual vacuum. And what else could fill this vacuum but naked power? When the armed forces struck in one country after another within the first decade of Independence it wasn't the result of a specific programme but a failure of ideas. Authoritarian rule will only end in Africa when new ideas, African ideas, begin to determine the limits of power and the nature of political institutions. This is necessarily a long and painful process. In the case of Nigeria it has meant two abortive civilian administrations, a bloody civil war, and nineteen years of military rule. The distinguished Nigerian writer, Wole Soyinka, saw this clearly enough in the early 1970's. In his prison journal, *The Man Died*, he prophesied with uncanny accuracy the likely tendency of Nigerian society in the aftermath of the civil war:

> Militarist entrepreneurs and multiple dictatorships: this is bound to be the legacy of a war which is conducted on the present terms. The vacuum in the ethical base . . . will be filled by a new military ethic – coercion. And the elitist formulation of the army, the entire colonial hangover which is sustained by the lack of national revaluation will itself maintain and promote the class heritage of society. The ramifications of the alliance of a corrupt and rapacious Mafia in society are endless and nearly incurable. The war means a consolidation of crime,

an acceptance of the scale of values that created the conflict, indeed an allegiance and enshrinement of that scale of values because it is now intimately bound in the sense of national identity.

And yet it was in Nigeria, where I attended the 'Symposium on African Literatures in Honour of Wole Soyinka', that I also saw the beginning of new possibilities.

2

> I love my country I no go lie
> Na inside am I go live and die
> I know my country I no go lie
> Na im and me go yap till I die.
>
> Wole Soyinka: *Etike Revo Wetin?*

In a way it was unfair of Tommy Thompson to compare Ghana with Nigeria, countries so wide apart in terms of wealth, population and sheer energy as to constitute almost different worlds. But he was right. It was at the Symposium – sponsored, ironically enough, by the military government – that I heard Soyinka tell the army in Africa to get out of politics and stay out. In his key-note address, 'Power and Creative Strategies', he demanded that his fellow-writers 'use their skill and exploit whatever strategies can be thought of for ending the uncertainty of social existence which is innate to the condition of the forcibly governed'; and added:

A few months ago, I seized my opportunity to call for the abolition of the theocratic ideal in all forms of government . . . Today, I seize the occasion to invite the writers of this continent to join me in a complementary endeavour. The 'divine right of kings' which ended with the decapitation of crowned heads of Europe several centuries ago, has – need I

14

state the obvious? – been replaced by the 'divine right of the gun' on this continent. We must now invite all our dictatorships, under no matter what camouflage, and however comparatively civilianised and domesticated they are – to set a definitive date *within this century* for the abandonment of this denigration of our popular will.

Fighting words, to be sure; this and more was said in front of the country's second-in-command, Rear-Admiral Augustus Aikhomu, who sat on the podium looking increasingly alarmed. It may even have crossed Aikhomu's mind that such an unambiguous call to arms might be translated by the assembled delegates into immediate action, in which case his neck would certainly have been on the line; and there was no mistaking the look of relief that crossed his features when the critical moment passed.

As the country's only Nobel laureate Soyinka was, of course, unassailable, a fact of which both he and Aikhomu were only too well aware. A less prominent person might have run into trouble. It is always foolish to underestimate any military government, especially in Nigeria, and this despite the present regime's continual pronouncements regarding the necessity for a human rights policy, which may be no more than a useful public relations exercise.

There is still the suspicion, for instance, that it is the present administration which is responsible for the assassination of Dele Giwa, the editor of the weekly *Newswatch* magazine, who was killed in October, 1986, by a parcel bomb delivered to his home three days after he was visited by senior security officers. According to rumour (I say *rumour*, since no-one has been charged there has yet to be a denial) Dele Giwa was told by one Gloria Okon, whom he had visited in London, that the wife of a certain person at the highest level was implicated in the escalating cocaine trade. No names need be mentioned, but every Nigerian journalist – every Nigerian – knows perfectly well who is being referred to. At any rate Dele Giwa was working on his article when he was murdered. Since then his lawyer, Chief Gani Fawehinmi, has been blocked at every turn by the police in his attempt to uncover the truth. He has been repeatedly detained on the flimsiest excuses, most recently in June this year. On more than one occasion he has publicly expressed fears for his life.

More recently still, a West Indian lecturer who had lived in Nigeria for twelve years, Patrick Wilmot, was kidnapped by the authorities on his way home one evening, driven overnight to Lagos airport and forcibly put on a flight to London. The authorities claimed that Wilmot, who had lived in Nigeria for twelve years and was married to a Nigerian, was a South African spy. In fact Wilmot, who is a self-avowed Marxist – a dangerous admission in the present climate, as another lecturer, Festus Iyayi, recently discovered – had published a list of Nigerian companies, some of them headed by prominent Government ministers, which were trading illegally with South Africa. If there was any substance to the charges against him he could have been brought before a court of law. The failure to institute proper proceedings – in effect breaking the law of the country – was already sufficient grounds for questioning the charge.

Yet, for all that, what was notable while I was in Lagos was the prominence Soyinka's address received in the following day's newspapers. Even the government-owned *Daily Times*, hardly famous for its radical journalism, quoted from it extensively on the front page. More amusing still was to hear the staff at the National Theatre – the bartender and the waiter and the doorman – loudly discussing, with undisguised approval, the import of what Soyinka had said. This, incidentally, gave the lie to the increasingly widespread notion, in Nigerian literary circles, that Soyinka is irrelevant to 'the masses' because he is too 'elitist'. His address might have been couched in his (sometimes) tortured phraseology, but 'the masses' didn't appear to have much trouble understanding it.

Such wide coverage of so damning a speech could never have occurred in Ghana where, only recently, a highly respected historian, Professor Adu Boahen, delivered a series of lectures at a public venue in Accra in which he castigated the Rawlings regime for subverting the society on the grounds that military rule *per se* was inimical to progress. Referring specifically to the present culture of silence in which the independent press has been 'strangulated', he spoke of the resultant climate of fear that had been generated in the country:

> We are afraid of being detained, liquidated or dragged before the CVC (Citizens Vetting Committee) or the NIC (National Investigations Committee) or being subjected to all sorts of molestations.

He also called for more equity and justice, for the restoration of freedom of association, and for the release of all political detainees.

Although the professor was not invited for questioning or in any way physically harmed (not yet, at any rate), the treatment his lectures received in the Ghanaian press was in contrast to the Nigerian example. An 'editorial' in *The Graphic*, for instance, claimed that Adu Boahen had 'at one time or another tried and failed in national politics', and then went on to say that his lectures were 'full of mischief and provocation', as though there was a logical and therefore damning connection between these two statements.

The attempt to slur a person's character in order to undermine their argument can only ever be expressed in the crudest terms, but what always seems to escape those who try to do so is the all-too obvious hysteria which only succeeds in defeating their purpose. One's instinctive reaction is always to disbelieve them, especially when they then proceed to engage in what amounts to a public vendetta: one week later, still apparently unable to leave the matter alone, the same paper carried a speech by a high-ranking military officer, General Quainoo, who repudiated the idea that the army was responsible for Ghana's present malaise and instead blamed those 'whose utterances and deeds showed that they are no patriots', the implication being that army generals are in the best position to decide who qualifies as a patriot and who doesn't. It goes without saying that their own patriotism is not in doubt, even if they continue to remain in power against the wishes of the citizens by virtue only of their imported military hardware. General Quainoo's speech was also carried in the *Ghanaian Times* over four consecutive days. Both reports, or editorials, or whatever they choose to call them, ended with what amounted to a death threat – or something that comes suspiciously close to one – against Professor Boahen, as follows:

> . . . if those who engineer division and national disintegration, financiers behind the mercenary plots, and instigators of tribalism do not put an end to their nefarious and subversive activities, what will come next time will not be fire but an inferno, a conflagration.

Unfortunately for the General, all this was rather late in the day. The lectures created a sensation in Accra, and this despite the fact that advertisements already paid for by the organisers failed to appear in any of the newspapers. On each of the three days of the lectures the spacious hall was packed to capacity. Those who couldn't get in gathered outside to listen on the public address system. And those who missed them altogether had no problem getting hold of the typescript, which ran to over seventy pages. It took me just twenty-four hours after arriving in Accra to locate a copy.

Later, in Liberia, an innocuous speech by yet another prominent academic, this time reported in one of the local newspapers, resulted in an invitation to the Executive Mansion for the ubiquitous 'interview'. Acquiring a copy of this speech proved more problematical, but the newspaper report, 'United States Blamed for Disunity among African States', gives a good idea of its content:

> As the Organisation of African Unity (OAU) observes its 25th anniversary, a Liberian professor has blamed the United States Government for disunity among African countries.
> He said when the late President Kwame Nkrumah of Ghana

proposed to his colleagues an all-African Union Government, the United States launched a campaign to discourage the idea.

Professor Elbert Dunn, acting chairman of the Political Science Department of the University of Liberia, was speaking in the auditorium of the University of Liberia last Friday during a colloquium organised by the Foreign Ministry as part of activities marking the OAU's 25th anniversary . . .

Professor Dunn said the United States Government convinced several African leaders that a united 'African Government' would be led by socialists and pro-Soviets, including Nkrumah and Nasser.

He said the United States also wrote to their allies in Africa warning them that such a union would introduce Communism to Africa . . .

Daily Observer, 23 May 1988

Innocuous, that is, until one understands the position of Liberia vis-a-vis the United States, but it would take a separate and much longer essay to explore the ramifications of foreign interference in the continent, and the way in which that interference, blatant in the extreme, encourages the most vicious regimes. As regards the United States and Liberia, we can say that America has landing and refuelling rights for military aircraft on twenty-four-hour notice; that private American investment in Liberia amounts to more than half a billion dollars; and that Liberia is the largest recipient of US economic aid in sub-Saharan Africa, including, in 1986, $2.9 million for the military alone.

And it was in Liberia, where I had gone after Ghana, that the full implication of Soyinka's speech and its subsequent coverage in the national dailies began to make sense in terms of the wider politics of West Africa. This came about largely through a chance meeting with a young Nigerian businessman who occupied the room next to mine in the Lebanese-run hotel in central Monrovia.

I use 'businessman' in the widest sense. Tall and thin with

19

delicate features, Remi knocked on my door early one morning and asked me if I had any foreign currency I wanted to change. When I told him my name and he learnt that my father was Nigerian he fell to talking. He told me that he had graduated a couple of years ago but hadn't been able to find a job; that after fruitlessly applying to one government department after another he had decided to do a little buying and selling; and that he was presently in Monrovia attempting to sell spare parts to the city's bus company. It seemed that South Korea had donated one hundred and fifty buses to the Liberian government as part of an aid package, but more than a hundred of these buses were now standing idle in the bus depot.

'These people are so stupid. Nobody could think of getting on a plane to buy spare parts. Meanwhile there's no public transport in the city and half the people you see walking about are unemployed.

'Liberians think small. They just want to make one dollar here, one dollar there. I couldn't believe it when I first came. But why should that concern me? I went to see the person responsible and told him to give me a list of what he needed together with exact specifications. Then I went back to my people in Nigeria and they made the parts for me. It was very simple. We can make anything in Nigeria. We have four steel mills in that country. Each one of them is bigger than this whole city.'

I've quoted him at some length because he conveys something of the energy of Nigerians, who were everywhere I went: in that hotel alone I counted twenty, all doing business of one kind or another. Later that evening, as we stood on the balcony watching the hookers walking up and down the main street, he pointed out three other hotels in the immediate vicinity which were patronised exclusively by Nigerians. 'Without Nigerians they would close tomorrow morning.' He fell silent for a moment, then he said,

'Our governments have failed us. Nigeria should be a great country but we have only succeeded in squandering our potential. Whatever you try to do they block you. We have all the expertise we need and yet we still haven't built our own car. Instead our leaders divide contracts between themselves to import foreign cars so they can buy houses in London. What we need in that country is a revolution. How many are we? One hundred and twenty million? Up to forty million can die and we will still be a big country. I give them five years and then we will drag them onto the street and deal with them.'

It is important in this context that he had no political axe to grind. He couldn't have been less interested in politics. He didn't care which regime was in power, or what ideology it subscribed to. In Africa the power struggle is not between contending ideologies but between governments and the people, between what can be loosely called the public and the private sectors. The public sector includes everyone in the bureaucratic set-up, from the journalists on the *Daily Graphic* to the officials at the checkpoints to the President himself; the private sector includes Remi and those Nigerian businessmen in Monrovia and the small traders I met everywhere. It was what a friend of mine meant when she said to me, 'In Europe you can ignore politics; here in Africa politics is with us all the time.' She didn't simply mean that life was uncertain, that it was possible to wake up one morning and suddenly discover that a coup had taken place overnight. She meant it in a wider and more literal sense, that whatever administration you had it imposed itself on you at every level of your life. Ideologies are irrelevant. The habit of dividing the continent into opposing political camps, which has become so engrained as to seem self-evident, is entirely mischievous. The only useful function it serves is to distort Africa's perception of itself for the purposes of foreign domination, otherwise known as neo-colonialism. The consequences are far more damaging than the price paid for raw materials, which is merely the end result.

Remi desired only to be left alone to provide for his family. Nor did he strike me as particularly greedy, and he was self-evidently prepared to work hard for what he wanted. But the little profit he had begun to make was being eaten up by officials, by all the petty functionaries he had to bribe along the way and the unfair competition from those higher up who had access to the big markets by virtue of their political positions.

'We will drag them onto the street and deal with them', he had said. He was not speaking lightly or indulging in bravado for its own sake. In Nigeria, the officials were more circumspect in the way they demanded money, and for good reason. Only last November, Lagos was brought to a standstill for three days when the populace, angered by the indiscriminate shooting of two brothers in broad daylight, went on the rampage and beat up every policeman they could lay their hands on. Police were seen to disappear into houses and emerge in civilian clothes. It took a military operation to restore order.

This was not the first time a Nigerian city had exploded so suddenly and with such violence. Figures are difficult to come by, but perhaps the worst riot occurred in the northern city of Kano in 1980. The Maitatsine Disturbances, so-called after the religious leader of that name, brought the city to a standstill for three weeks and resulted in more than four thousand deaths. To date, the army has largely been spared the public wrath, but the alacrity with which successive military regimes have set a timetable for the return to civilian rule strongly suggests that they are only too well-aware of the fragility of their own position. Listening to the young businessman, and judging from the response to Soyinka's address, it didn't seem too fanciful to conclude that their hour may have come round at last.

In fact it almost happened while I was there. The country was on the brink of a general strike following the recent hike in petrol prices and there was much talk, in taxis, in bars, among friends and acquaintances, of the coming showdown. Already the authorities had moved to close twenty universities following student disturbances, and for one tense weekend, which included a Bank Holiday Monday, nobody knew what would happen. The President himself refused to appear on television, and privately people were calling for his resignation.

Who's afraid of Wole Soyinka?

Power in Africa – to put it at its crudest – amounts to nothing more than legalised theft, a fact which is rammed home every time an officer drives past in a brand-new Mercedes. Everybody knows the gap between the officer's salary and the price of the car. They also know that there is an intimate connection between that officer's Mercedes and their own hunger. But to know a thing is not enough in itself. I met any number of people in Ghana and Liberia and Sierra Leone who knew perfectly well the source of the problem, but that was where it ended. There was never any hint that they could change it; they assumed that it would continue to be this way. They were helpless in the face of something far more powerful than themselves. How many times did I hear the words, 'We suffer too much in Africa?', and yet the tone was invariably one of resignation. God had decreed it so, and so it must be. This has nothing to do with elaborate theories of indigenous African thought processes so beloved by European anthropologists. Human beings, everywhere, can get used to anything, even tyranny. Life is then reduced to the simple level of personal survival; all else is extraneous.

Nigeria was the exception, and it explains Remi's uncharitable irritation with Liberians. He was expressing something far deeper than impatience with a people who seemed to him incapable of determining their own affairs, even over the small matter of whether or not they had functioning buses. Two small scenarios come to mind, unimportant in themselves but with far-reaching ramifications.

I made the mistake of travelling from Lagos to Accra by Nigeria Airways. As usual there was complete chaos at the check-in counter. Tempers flared and a fight seemed likely although it was difficult to work out, above the shouting and the shoving, exactly who was arguing with whom, or why. A passing soldier, his AK 47 slung over his shoulder, attempted to intervene. This turned out to be a mistake on his part. The argument was quickly forgotten as the intending passengers, at each other's throats only a moment ago, suddenly turned on him.

I'm not in the habit of feeling sorry for soldiers, but the look of bewilderment on the man's face as he retreated in confusion was enough to excite anybody's sympathy.

Later, in Cote d'Ivoire, I wanted to change a traveller's cheque in order to buy a ticket to Monrovia. It was a Saturday and the banks were shut. Someone suggested I try the Hotel Ivoire, the most expensive hotel in Abidjan and notorious in West Africa as the only hotel in the region with an ice rink. I had with me a Ghanaian with whom I had travelled from Accra the previous day, and who had been kind enough to give me a bed for the night when he discovered that I knew nobody in the city.

'Are you a resident?' the man behind the counter asked. I shook my head. 'Then I can't change it.' I knew he was just being obstreperous, which is the way of officials in Africa, but before I could remonstrate with him my companion started pleading,

'Please, I'm begging you . . .'

At the risk of labouring the point, it is easy to see the way in which the Ghanaian's knee-jerk reaction towards authority helps to perpetuate tyranny by a subtle process of collaboration in which power is invested with a mystique that it can't otherwise possess. There is nothing intrinsically mysterious about a pair of dark glasses and well-polished boots over and above your own irrational responses. Nigerians didn't need Soyinka to give intellectual respectability to what they already knew, ie: that a uniform is just a uniform, but the fact that he did so wasn't lost on that hostile group at the Nigeria Airways check-in counter. If I were forced to make a prediction I would say that military rule is on its way out in Nigeria, at least in its present form, and that this represents the greatest hope for the rest of the continent. With almost one-quarter of Africa's population, including one-third of its children, Nigeria is the powerhouse of the continent. And when a person starts selling you spare parts for your buses you can be sure that the ideas which produced those spare parts are included in the package: a job-lot, so to speak.

May 1988

24

Postscript: strategies for survival

Nigeria is held together by a balance of terror
Alhaji Balarabe Musa

In October last year I was a guest at the Centre for West African Studies in Birmingham University. I was there to read my work and field questions from the audience. I took along with me some copies of *Index on Censorship* in the hope of winning a few subscribers. I didn't know that the Nigerians in the audience were familiar with the magazine, still less that they had read my article on the journey I undertook to five West African countries a few months before.

In that article, 'Who's afraid of Wole Soyinka?', I tried to suggest a qualitative difference between Nigeria and the other countries in the region. This difference was reflected in terms of Nigeria's size, wealth and cultural diversity; but it was the forces released in the society by these factors that struck me, specifically the powerful interest groups which between them maintained a check on the official excesses of a Liberia, say, or a Sierra Leone. And this in spite of the present regime's current crackdown on 'extremists'.

The occasion of my insight was a government-sponsored symposium on African Literature held at the National Theatre in Lagos to honour the award of the Nobel prize to Soyinka. Unfortunately for the authorities, represented at the opening session by the President's second-in-command, the great playwright used the opportunity to tell the soldiers to stop interfering in the nation's politics: 'We must now invite all our dictatorships, under no matter what camouflage, and however comparatively civilianised and domesticated they are – to set a definitive date *within this century* for the abandonment of this denigration of the popular will.'

All the Nobel prizes in the world wouldn't have protected Soyinka's Liberian counterpart, but then the nihilism of Liberian

25

society, and with it the dearth of any opposition (however enfeebled), precludes the same level of intellectual activity which produces a Nobel prize-winner in the first place. Soyinka didn't emerge out of a vacuum; his achievement must be measured against the background of the nation's creative output over the last thirty years; and in his address to the Symposium he was only fulfilling his function in terms of the larger group which he represented at that moment.

The Nigerian intelligentsia is amongst the most powerful of the interested parties presently contending for the country's future. Literally so: Nigerians are perfectly well aware that time is no longer the elastic commodity it was at Independence in 1960. The only available options for the country are greatness or collapse, and each day that passes without resolution in the direction of the former makes the latter more certain. It is as stark as this, and the fault lies squarely with successive administrations – military *and* civilian – whose paralysing lack of vision has translated power into tyranny.

Confronted with this polarisation one's duty is clear: 'If we didn't take on the government we couldn't see who else would.' The words are those of Dr Festus Iyayi, who was in London recently to pick up the Commonwealth prose prize for his latest novel. The award was the culmination of an eventful year in which he was dismissed from his university post, and then held for a month without charge or trial following a strike by the Academic Staff Union of Universities.

The fact of Iyayi's incarceration is less interesting than his own perceived role within the life of the society. The stakes are high in Nigeria. 'He played with the big boys and he lost,' a friend said to me when Dele Giwa, the investigative journalist, was murdered by a letter bomb delivered to his house by two unidentified men in October, 1986. My friend was right. His personal feelings concerning Giwa's exposure of the stench in everybody's nostrils ('Stifled, O days! O lands! in every public and private corruption!') were not at issue here, only the realities of contemporary Nigerian society. However: ' "It is the eve of Dele Giwa's murder," the fellow screamed into the cold night, "so let nobody come and lecture me about fundamental human rights until his murderers have been caught." '

This is taken from an article, 'Rites of Passage', which appeared in a recent issue of *Newswatch*, the Lagos-based weekly magazine which Giwa founded twelve months before his death. The author, Adebayo Williams, a regular contributor who happened to be at my reading session in Birmingham, records what preceded the outburst:

'It was by all means an engrossing and enjoyable evening; or so it seemed until the subject of the abridgment of human rights by the Pinochets of Africa reared its monstrous head. Maja-Pearce was asked for one on-the-spot assessment of the situation in Africa. Our man had reeled off the names of several African countries over which the dark clouds of censorship and intolerance hung.

"What about Nigeria?" snarled a fierce-looking Nigerian who had been swinging uneasily on his chair.

"Nigeria is okay," Maja-Pearce noted rather casually.

"I'm surprised you can say that," the Nigerian snapped. He was about to storm out of the place when I restrained him.

Maja-Pearce then went ahead to buttress his claim that fundamental human rights were still largely respected in Nigeria. He had cited as an example the freedom and independence of the Nigerian press. He had been particularly impressed by the daring and courage of Wole Soyinka's thunderous address to the writers' symposium in May, while a glum-faced Admiral Aikhomu sat through the epic dressing-down. This could only take place in Nigeria, observed Maja-Pearce, obviously unaware of Balarabe Musa's perceptive theory of the balance of terror . . .

Our Nigerian gladiator could, however, not be impressed by Pearce's explanation which he privately dismissed as the rhetorics of deceit and ignorance typical of Nigerian journalists.'

The outburst which followed wasn't in itself as dramatic as one might be inclined to think. Nigerians are a volatile people who express themselves forcefully, as witness Adebayo Williams' own strong – and quite deliberate – use of language: the evening is 'engrossing and enjoyable'; Soyinka's speech is 'daring and courageous'; the 'fierce-looking Nigerian' snaps and snarls. Everything happens on a big scale, including what might seem a rather trivial event to those who come from less vociferous – or less fractured – societies: I don't recall any raised voices during the exchange, or the tussle which he claims ensued.

Journalists in Britain use words in their literal meaning; journalists in Nigeria use words as camouflage: Adebayo Williams' language, which is no more than standard Nigerian journalese, serves a purpose beyond his dramatic account of an unimportant event in a British city one wet October evening. The drama in this instance is a deliberate strategy to take sides in the hottest issue on the Nigerian political scene: human rights.

When the current administration seized power in a palace coup in August, 1985, it did so on a human rights platform: 'Fundamental rights and civil liberties will be respected,' the new President announced in his maiden broadcast, and ever since then he has been doing his best to outstrip his predecessors in this regard. Only recently, eleven workers at the National Electric Power Authority were sentenced to life imprisonment on a charge of 'economic sabotage',* ie, participating in a three-day strike; at this moment, five members of the Bankers' Union are being held in detention for a strike which never even took place.

Against this background one treads carefully, and journalists who wish to add a dissenting voice declare their positions with the memory of 'the first martyr of modern Nigerian journalism' very much in mind. Adebayo Williams sympathises with the seething Nigerian at the same time as he endorses Balarabe Musa's 'perceptive theory of the balance of terror', but he has done so only by implication. This may be no more than a useful holding operation, but in the longer term it will be too late for everybody, the power-brokers included. In passing, he takes the

28

opportunity to gloat once again over Aikhomu's 'epic dressing-down'; and it is this demystification of power, the determination to see beyond the Admiral's uniform and the truckload of armed soldiers that accompanied him to a literary event (but this is Nigeria), which is itself part of the check on tyranny.

*They were subsequently 'pardoned' in December 1990.

Fear and loathing in Lagos*

On my second night in Lagos there was an armed robbery in the next compound. The Indian family who lived there managed to escape across the rooftop and over the wall before the gang finally broke through the steel door and made off with a consignment of video recorders, but the nightguard was shot dead attempting to defend himself with a home-made bow and arrow. The police, who had been notified by phone in good time, finally turned up in a battered Land Rover as dawn was breaking. They weren't even apologetic about the fact that they had taken five hours to drive two miles, but nobody was surprised by what was, after all, a familiar enough demonstration of official incompetence. Perhaps – who knows? – they were themselves implicated in the affair. One hears too many stories about police complicity in armed robbery, and I knew for a fact that buying a gun from the police's own arsenal was only a matter of money, preferably in hard currency.

Segun, my old school-friend with whom I stayed, owned a gun. He kept it in a wooden box under his bed. On the night of the robbery he and his brother, who lived in the adjoining bungalow, made a great show of patrolling their compound with weapons at the ready while their wives calmed the children and brewed coffee. This was frontier life in a modern city, but to live in Lagos is to live in a constant state of seige, and not only in your own house. It's perfectly possible to be robbed at knifepoint on a main street in broad daylight, or to have your car snatched from you in one of the city's interminable go-slows. In either case it would be fatal to fight back. The fact that armed robbery carries a mandatory death sentence by firing squad – without appeal – has merely succeeded in raising the stakes. It's not surprising that diplomatic staff have been known to jeopardise their careers by refusing a post in Lagos, or that Reuters news agency asks its correspondents to stay only two years instead of the usual three.

To say that Lagos is anarchic is merely to repeat what every visitor has said before you. The only wonder is that the city continues to function at all. The authorities for their part, who can't ensure a working telephone system or a continuous water supply or uninterrupted electricity, are forever trying to demonstrate that they really are in control. Occasionally they succeed; mostly they fail. I was greatly relieved, when I entered the country this time, to be confronted at the airport by a scene of perfect order. Someone later explained that the government, in characteristic military fashion, had issued a 'shoot at sight' directive against the beggars, touts and criminals who made the place an absolute nightmare for the traveller. It seems that matters had got so out of hand that only a few weeks earlier an aircraft from a neighbouring African country had been stormed by an armed gang as it taxied on the runway and then stripped bare before the officials realised what had happened. For a government which is anxious to encourage foreign investment, and therefore foreign businessmen, such an affront to their authority couldn't be tolerated.

But this was the exception. More often than not, such exercises usually add to the existing confusion. For instance, while I was in Lagos there was a sudden crackdown on illegal motorists. No announcement was made, but then no-one ever expects to be told these things in advance. It just happened that one morning road blocks appeared at all the major junctions and remained there for a full week. The authorities subsequently claimed that a number of stolen vehicles were recovered in the course of the operation, but that was only half the story. 'Where your paper?' could equally refer to the colour of your money as your car registration or insurance or even your driving licence. 'N5 will do,' Segun said to me when we were stopped at yet another roadblock late one evening. For someone like me, with a pocketful of hard currency, this was an absurdly small sum; but judging by the policeman's response – 'Thank you, sir, I'm grateful' – one mightn't have guessed that it represented less than the price of twenty cigarettes.

The police were doubtless pleased with their unexpected pre-Christmas bonus, which might have been the whole point of the exercise, but all it meant for the travelling public was even more hardship in a city already notorious for its traffic jams. Lagos proper, the commercial heart of the city, is an island four square miles in area which is joined to the mainland by a series of bridges. This means that there are long queues in one direction every morning and in the other direction every evening. The only people who benefit from the results of such an awkward geography are the street hawkers, some as young as eight or nine, who will run half-a-mile across the scorching tarmac to sell you a bar of chocolate.

Nor were matters helped by the sudden shortage of communal taxis, the main form of public transport in a city with an inadequate bus service and no rail network. Many of the taxis were presumably illegal and therefore off the road for the duration. Those that continued to ply for trade naturally took advantage of simple market economics to increase their fares. Lagos taxi drivers are belligerent enough at the best of times (so would you be if you drove a taxi in Lagos), but there was an added aggression in the 'Na two naira,' as though to say: If you don't like it you can always walk. And many did walk, ten miles or more every day, because there was little point waiting for an overloaded 1950's Bedford bus that would probably break down before you reached your destination.

Sometimes, when I was too tired to fight it out or I was simply late for an appointment, I would charter a taxi to myself by standing a little to one side of the crowd and shouting 'Drop!' at the top of my voice. It was well worth the fifteen or twenty naira –

one pound fifty pence at most – which was easily more than a day's wage for the ordinary worker. It was also more than the taxi driver would earn if he carried the regulation four passengers at the normal fare. But why, I wondered, looking at the sheer frustration on the faces around me, did the people put up with this? Why did they tolerate the blatant injustice which deprived three of them of an already scarce commodity only because I had more money than they did?

The reason is money itself; or, rather, an attitude towards money which dominates the society to the exclusion of all else. People in Lagos are judged only by what they have, not who they are. The person who drives a Mercedes is better than the person who drives a Peugeot, and the person who drives a Rolls Royce – the latest fad, even in these stringent economic times – is better than either. The subtle gradations of a more settled society – family, class, breeding – are entirely alien, and for good historical reasons. Until the beginning of the nineteenth century Lagos, which today has a population of about seven million, was a sparsely-populated coastal settlement. Because of its natural harbour it was annexed by the British as a trading post for the goods of the interior. The city expanded with trade, which was the only reason for its existence; but the colonial experience itself, the fracture with the past and the consequent spiritual vacuum that comes with the loss of identity, generated the very mercantile values which ensured its success. It was a city of merchants, many of whom, like the freed Brazilian slaves in search of their roots – Marinho, Cardoso, Da Silva: I went to school with their descendants – quickly discovered that obscure longings could be satisfied by bricks and mortar. The result of their building spree can be seen in the proliferation of Port-uguese-style architecture in the older areas of the city.

But if money is an end in itself then anything goes, including armed robbery and police corruption, both of which are only different aspects of the underlying brutality of a society which recognises no other values. One of my most enduring memories as a child was the sight of my father punching the cook repeatedly because his food wasn't ready on time. My father wasn't a wicked man, just a man who lived his life by the ethos of his society; fifteen years later, on my first return to Lagos, it was distressing to see Segun behave in a similar way, this time towards the housemaid. He used a switch instead of his fist, and he didn't draw blood, but it was the inability to recognise the other's humanity which overrode the squalid details in either case: both the cook and the housemaid might as well have been commodities purchased in the open market, which is effectively what they were.

And yet even I failed to realise the extent of the problem until, quite inadvertently, Segun suddenly revealed the true nature of his relationship with his wife. It happened on my last visit. We had been drinking with a mutual friend of ours, also a former classmate, whose printing firm was on the verge of bankruptcy. Later, as we were driving home, Segun said: 'The trouble with Toyin is that he doesn't discuss his business affairs with his wife. After all, if he can't trust her then who can he trust?' I was surprised to hear him say this, but he had got it wrong. Toyin's tragedy was much simpler: he was an intellectual, not a business-man, a condition which amounted to a personality defect in terms of the society in which he was forced to make a living. He would have been happier lecturing at a university or working on a newspaper, but he was trapped by the pressure from family and friends (but mostly family, of the extended variety) to stay in the business he had inherited from his father and make his fortune. But I didn't say any of this to Segun. Instead, I muttered something to the effect that Toyin's wife seemed like a nice woman; whereupon he said, as casually as though it were self-evident: 'I don't believe that a woman is either good or bad; I believe that a woman is what you make her.'

'I believe that a woman is what you make her' – Men, everywhere, are given to uttering all manner of puerile state-ments about women, but there was no reason to think that he was merely repeating a sentiment that sounded smart to the upwardly mobile male Lagos bourgeoisie. Nor did he appear conscious of the implications of what he had just said. He meant it. And, after all, it was entirely logical. If life was to be judged only in material terms, it followed that the worth of a human being – any human being, from the housemaid upwards – was in direct proportion to their relative power in the money stakes. Tola, his wife (let us at least give her a name), could produce babies and help him in his practice and she could be equally efficient at both without in any way challenging his reductive vision of the world. The point is that neither activity depended on her moral autonomy. In effect she was just a better-educated housemaid.

Human beings were commodities, period. There was no higher idea of a person's worth outside their monetary value. Women, naturally, got the bad end of the deal, as the men never tired of demonstrating. Take someone like Gbadebo, another classmate of mine and now a successful doctor. Success for him didn't mean being a good doctor but making lots of money. This in turn meant filling his twenty-bed clinic, a graduation present from his parents, with a succession of wealthy clients who were rarely ill enough to warrant hospitalisation. Gbadebo would simply put them on a course of aspirin, take a few x-rays, and then present them with an outrageous bill at the end of a fortnight. The 'patients' themselves worked on the assumption that the more you paid, the better your treatment, so both parties were satisfied.

Meanwhile, on the street outside, children were dying of every imaginable disease under the tropical sun. In fact Gbadebo wasn't into medicine so much as public relations, the sole object of which was money: 'the betrayal of vocation for the attractions of power in one form or another,' was the way that Wole Soyinka, the Nobel laureate, characterised the phenomenon as far back as the early 1970's.

And what did Gbadebo do with all the money that he made? He took two or three holidays a year, usually in London, where he would put up in an expensive hotel and do the rounds of the nightclubs in order to fuck as many women as possible. And 'fuck' was the operative verb: women were only the means of a slightly less solitary form of masturbation, which is what it amounted to. And that was all that London represented. The suggestion that he go to an art gallery or the theatre or a concert would have met with a bewildered: What for? Indeed; his only other activity, accomplished in the space of an afternoon, was to buy a gross of the old school tie to sell to the clerk with whom he had an arrangement.

This was the sum total of Gbadebo's life, which was presumably why his wife left him after they had been married only a year. One day she simply packed her things and went – all the way to New York, in fact – taking their daughter with her. But she was lucky, and not only because she had the means to assert her worth as a human being. It would be difficult to overestimate her courage in a society where a woman is considered to be the property of her husband: a man who decides to 'sack' his wife (like: 'I sacked my housemaid') is automatically awarded custody of the children. The estranged wife, who is suddenly reduced to the level of a poor relation in a relative's household, is then expected to send emissaries to 'beg' her husband. He may or may not grant her access to the children; at any rate, his word is final. This was the fate of my father's first wife. She had lived for years in an alien climate while he studiously plotted his career as a big man, but when she died, in a rented room somewhere in Lagos, she hadn't even saved enough for a decent burial.

'I could never buy a house with my wife's money,' Segun said one day. 'This is my house, I paid for it. Whenever she wants anything she only has to ask me. If I have it I give her; if I don't have it, I tell her that I don't have it. What I can't afford she does without. Finish.' The unspoken, 'any nonsense and she's out', doesn't have to mean that you then proceed to actually treat her like a housemaid – Segun was a considerate man in many ways – but it is intolerable, after all, for a person's happiness to be wholly dependent on someone else's sense of propriety. Gbadebo's wife couldn't be doing with it so she got out; but if it was necessary for her to travel all the way to the United States it was because she knew very well that her life would have been miserable in Lagos.

A woman who rejects her 'place' is to be pitied and despised because her example challenges all the self-serving notions about what it means to be a man.

As for Gbadebo, his wife's departure meant that he could now work his way through the student nurses in the hostel across the way with the full encouragement and sympathy of all those who professed themselves perplexed by her self-evidently unreasonable behaviour. And he didn't even have to worry about all those little comforts that a man in his position might otherwise be expected to miss. He had a houseboy, a youth of eighteen, who washed his clothes and made his bed and heated his food for him at two in the morning. It was easy enough to see how one could be seduced by some aspects of the society, to shout at servants and hog taxis and generally have people bow and scrape only because you happen to be a man with money in your pocket. You didn't have to curb your temper or chase taxis with the crowd, you didn't even have to fetch a bottle of beer for yourself. It was a life of total indulgence. All you had to do was pay for it.

And paying for it was admittedly difficult. Segun especially worked hard for what he had. He took it as given that you put in a twelve-hour day and then stayed up all weekend to finish a report that was needed first thing Monday morning. There were no safety nets in the society, no national health service or state schools or mortgage facilities. You paid for everything up-front. If you didn't, or couldn't, then you ended up like the woman on the footbridge that I had to cross to catch a taxi to the city centre. She was always there, no matter what the time of day, always in the same faded-blue cotton dress, always with the baby held just so against the heat of the sun and the fumes from six lanes of traffic. She had nothing; her visible chances of survival were zero; but perhaps her case wasn't as desperate as that of the woman who was reduced to exposing her deformed left breast at one of the city's few functioning traffic lights. Don't talk about human dignity. Even a deformity was an asset in the fight for survival.

It's possible that certain ideas about human relations are the product of wealthy societies, and that my own responses towards Lagos are dictated by my years in Europe, but I doubt it. People, everywhere, hunger for more. When they deny the need they become neurotic. Gbadebo's behaviour was profoundly neurotic. He achieved his life only by denying what was most precious about it: his humanity; his sense of himself as a person in the world. He wasn't engaged at any but the most superficial level, which was why women could only be the objects of his urgent desire, so quickly satisfied, and why he thought nothing of the regular abortions he performed (free of charge, no less) on those women foolish enough to get caught. And what was true of him was true of the society as a whole. Every visitor to Lagos remarks on the sheer energy of the city and then reacts to it according to their temperament, but they hardly even see that this energy is negative, self-defeating, nihilistic. It produces nothing but chaos and confusion.

Chinua Achebe, the celebrated novelist, once described Lagos as 'the war front' and wondered why anybody bothered to live there. For me, of course, there is an added personal dimension, but then the landscape of one's childhood is at once too specific and too general. I could talk about the smell on the air just before a tropical rainstorm or the recollection of a fishing expedition on the lagoon at the bottom of our garden or the sound of crickets at night as I lay in bed, but none of this will help the casual visitor (or embassy staff) who must barricade themselves indoors after dark and bribe their way through roadblocks erected only because the powers-that-be have a need to exercise their fragile authority.

And, yet, I'm tempted to end with one final image which suggests that there may be more to the city than the sum total of the horrors described above. It isn't much in itself, just the sight of a young man attempting to sell footballs to frustrated motorists in a traffic jam. I was in a taxi at the time, and as frustrated as everybody else, but I remember the way he suddenly started dribbling between the cars as though he was participating in a game of basketball. There was real pleasure on his face, and I remember thinking that if such a man could indulge in play for its own sake then perhaps all was not lost. On the other hand, I may be reading too much into it for the sake of those childhood memories which make claims that go beyond my distress at what I see each time I return to Lagos. I don't know, and perhaps I never will, but whatever the case it can't possibly mitigate any of the foregoing: that one is observing a city under seige.

December 1989

*Originally published as 'Lagos: A City Under Seige', *Marie Claire*, June 1990.

Postscript: on patriots and patriotism

'The English are a nation of brutes and should be exterminated to the last man.' The words are those of a nineteenth-century Englishman, John Bright; the occasion was a dinner held in his honour at the American embassy in London. According to Henry Adams, in whose autobiography this appears, the Americans present were shocked that a leading politician should condemn his compatriots in such forthright terms – in front of foreigners. But the Americans, still insufficiently sure of their independence, were simply naive. John Bright, who didn't give a damn what foreigners thought, was sufficiently convinced of his nation's greatness to be able to abuse his countrymen when and how he pleased.

To paraphrase John Bright: Nigerians are a nation of brutes and should be exterminated to the last man – to say nothing of the last woman. This, at least, was the tenor of an essay on Lagos that I recently published in a British magazine, complete with the obligatory colour photographs showing the great mounds of uncollected garbage for which the city has become famous. In the process, I also took a swipe at the unbelievable philistinism of the Lagos bourgeoisie, their contempt for all moral and aesthetic values, which makes possible a level of brutality that can only be called barbaric.

Sure enough, the heavens fell. No sooner had the essay appeared than I received a phone call from a London-based Nigerian journalist, Omotayo Afolabi, demanding to know what I thought I was doing portraying 'our nation' in a 'negative light' for a 'foreign audience'. She went even further. In a libellous – not to say hysterical – article for a (London-based) Nigerian newspaper ('The bashing of Lagos', *Nigeria Home News*, 24–30 May 1990), she attempted to answer her own question:

> In my opinion he (Adewale Maja-Pearce) is playing up to the powers that lap up such derogatory material, otherwise you don't get published. Is it right to disgrace your nation for the pounds sterling you get in return? I wonder how much one gets paid for such trash? . . .
>
> Veteran journalist, Eddie Iroh, writing in *Newswatch*, describes Lagos as the ash-tray of British hack writers. They can add another to their fold. Only one of us. Or is he?

Ironically, I then received a letter from none other than our veteran journalist – the *oga* himself, so to speak: 'With all due modesty, some of us have written very deeply critical pieces about the problems of Nigeria, and done so over a longer time than you can match' – in which he informed me, with all due pomposity, that the payment I received for my 'misdirected social concern' was, in his considered opinion (so many opinions!), 'the moral equivalent of blood money'.

If Eddie Iroh is indeed the measure of Nigerian journalism, then we all have good reason to be worried, to wit:

> Can you point to any British journalist, indeed any foreign writer, even those in political exile, who has written with so

much venom against his own fatherland – in a foreign publication?

Modesty forbids me from giving him a lecture on the history of English literature – or Irish, or Mexican, or American, or . . . – even if I'm tempted to wonder why it is that these oh-so-patriotic exiles should themselves write articles, in the pages of this magazine, telling us all about the house they own 'three minutes' walk from Hyde Park. I think we all know something about prevailing exchange rates and London property prices, but let us leave that to one side. Amid all the talk of blood money, one might be tempted to speculate in unhealthy directions.

More sinister, perhaps, is the Big Brother syndrome unexpectedly revealed in the closing paragraph:

> Let me observe, in conclusion, that in your bitterness against everything Nigerian – *a fact well known to many of us* (my italics) – you even allowed emotion to override contemporary as well as historical facts.

Who, precisely, is this 'us'? And where are the 'facts'? For a 'veteran journalist' who has 'written very deeply about the problems of Nigeria', he conspicuously fails to provide a single example of the distortion he claims to find in my essay.

In this respect at least his acolyte fares slightly better. In her own article, Ms Afolabi doubts my veracity over an example I provide in support of my argument:

> Perhaps the images he describes exist more in the imagination than in reality. For he further says: 'One desperate case was that of a woman reduced to exposing her deformed left breast at one of the city's few functioning traffic lights. Even a deformity can be an asset in the fight for survival.' In all my stay in Nigeria, I've not come across such a sight.

I could point her in the direction of Ojuelegba Bus Stop, but this would miss the point. The levels of human misery one encounters on the streets of Lagos are rendered more obscene,

41

not less, by a squabble over whether or not a particular piece of evidence will stand up in a court of law; however: 'Even if it is the case,' she hastens to add, 'should a Nigerian take it upon himself to broadcast our ills for foreigners to laugh at?' Not a word about those unable even to rent a room in Ajegunle, much less buy a house in Hyde Park, only concern that the wretched figure in question, whose own invisibility turns out to be the price of that house, might render London-based Nigerian journalists the objects of ridicule in their adopted country: '. . . your audience in this article,' Mr Iroh concurs, 'is almost entirely British. You are thus giving comfort and entertainment at the expense of your own . . .'

So there we have it. Our veteran journalist's deep criticisms of his society stop well short of his concern that his neighbour in Hyde Park might come across my essay and thereby cause him discomfort. Such a shallow response to the problems of Nigeria can hardly be credited, which is presumably why he must attempt to forestall the uneasiness he might reasonably feel by resorting to that hoary old chestnut, colonialism:

> If Nigeria is a money and class society, what is Britain? And from whence that heritage? You see no link between British colonialism and contemporary Nigerian problems because you dismiss colonialism simply as a 'fracture with the past'. Haba! Adewale!

At a stroke, then (Haba! Eddie!), it turns out that his amused neighbour, three decades after decolonisation, is himself responsible for the sights that assail anybody who bothers to open their eyes to the obscenities of life in Lagos. Not a word about the fortune (Gowon: 'Our problem is not money but how to spend it') that those in positions of power and responsibility in the country – Nigerians, all of them – have squandered in order that the majority of its citizens should wonder where their next meal is coming from; not a word about the mansions on Victoria Island – Nigerian-owned, all of them – that mock the slums of Maroko. If foreigners do indeed laugh at Nigeria; if the country has become a by-word for graft and corruption on a scale rivalled only by the most decadent societies, then perhaps we might usefully ask ourselves why this is so, and ask it in a way which goes beyond the easy rhetoric of colonialism (always blame the other person), and in the process denies Nigerians the responsibility for their own destiny. Britain, at least, does not fool about with the lives of its children, which is presumably why any number of Nigerian journalists (and not only journalists: one quarter of a million, at the last count) have chosen to settle here. And they might also remember, as they take a walk in Hyde Park on a Sunday afternoon, that this is partly so because any number of her writers have considered it their patriotic duty to proclaim the ills of their society to anybody who will listen. We are, truly, a nation of brutes, who must cower before those to whom we have given the right to point the finger.

The mark of the beast:
Nigeria in the year 1989

Animal talk done start again:
'Dash them human rights'.
How animal go know say they no born me as slave?
How animal go know say slave trade don't pass?
And they want dash us human rights
. . . Human rights na my property
You can't dash me my property.

Fela Anikulapo-Kuti: Beasts of No Nation

1

I hadn't been able to reach Festus Iyayi on the phone. Getting any number outside Lagos was all-but impossible. In the end it was easier to undertake the four-hour journey by long-distance taxi to Benin and hope for the best. Such is the state of Nigeria in the year 1989. Thirty years of independence and you can't even make a phone call.

It was late when I arrived in Benin. I didn't have Festus' new home address so I put up in an hotel overnight, but when I arrived at his office in the morning I was told that he had just left for Lagos. I didn't then know about the ill-fated conference that was to be held the following day to discuss alternatives to the IMF-inspired austerity measures.

Known as the Structural Adjustment Programme (SAP), these measures included devaluation of the currency to ten per cent of its former value, the liberalisation of imports, mass re-entrenchment in the public sector, and cuts in the already pitiful welfare programmes. In return, Nigeria qualified once again for the loans that were needed to repay the interest on the outstanding loans, which were already consuming three-quarters of the country's foreign exchange earnings. One didn't need to be an economist to wonder at the wisdom of such a policy, particularly when one saw the human results on the streets of the capital, or heard about those with access to these loans sending their children to Swiss boarding schools. It wasn't surprising that there had been full-scale rioting only the previous month, and never mind what the government said about 'extremists', 'radicals' and 'subversive elements' causing confusion in the society.

If I had known about the 'Alternative to SAP' conference, in which Festus was to be one of the guest speakers, along with Chief Gani Fawehinmi, the radical lawyer; Dr Tai Solarin, the social critic; and Dr Michael Imoudu, the veteran labour activist, I would have hurried back to Lagos, where I would have witnessed a police exercise in public repression that has become a familiar feature of the regime of General Ibrahim Badamasi Babangida (IBB for short). Instead, I pushed further east, to Enugu, where I spent the night with Peter Ezeh. He is currently regional correspondent of *The Punch* and supplies us at *Index* with regular updates on the deteriorating state of the press. We had never previously met, and I wanted to take the opportunity to establish personal contact with him.

Peter was overjoyed to see me. He insisted on introducing me to his friends and colleagues as 'my important visitor from London', but it was my own admiration for his courage and integrity as a professional journalist which had brought me all this way. One of the tragedies of Nigeria is the extent to which a country of more than a hundred million people is held together only by the determination of a few individuals who take it upon themselves to challenge the recurring madness of successive regimes, military as well as civilian. It was easy enough for me to scuttle back to London and publish essays in *Index*. The worst the government could do was deny me a visa when I next applied to enter the country. That would be difficult enough at a personal level, but I wouldn't be imprisoned, or lose my job, or jeopardise the physical safety of my family.

Placing one's family in the firing line was always a possibility. It was in Peter's office, ironically enough, that I came across a report in that day's edition of *The Republic* which involved a crooked businessman, the number two in government, and large sums of money in a Swiss bank account. There was obviously going to be trouble, and so it happened: that same evening plain clothes policemen descended on the editor's house. When they didn't find him in they promptly arrested his wife. She was detained overnight, and only released when her husband reported to the police station in person the next day.

'Aikhomu in $3.5m scandal' (*The Republic*, 16 June, 1989) was innocuous enough in itself, but it followed a pattern about corruption in high places which was familiar to every Nigerian with the least interest in politics, which is to say every Nigerian. The report simply stated that lawyers from Chief Gani Fawehinmi's chambers had 'filed an exparte motion urging the Lagos High Court to compel the Inspector-General of Police to investigate allegations of corruption made by one Alhaji Muhamad Bashir against the Chief of General Staff, Vice-Admiral Augustus Aikhomu'. The article also included the name of the Swiss bank – Standard Chartered Bank, Zurich – as well as the account numbers – Personal Account Number 190: 788 152442; and Investment Account Number 391: 193 152441 – in which the money was alleged to have been deposited, and ended by quoting the lawyers to the effect that 'the Nigeria Police have a duty imposed on them under Section 4 of the Police Act, 1967, to investigate any complaint or allegation validly made against anybody in a position of importance'.

Nowhere did the report offer any comment on the allegation; nowhere did it speculate on whether the allegation was true or false. It merely reported an action filed before the High Court and, as such, already in the public domain. But this was sufficient reason for a detachment of armed police, complete with tear-gas canisters (just in case), to ransack the editor's house and seize his pregnant wife. This is obviously an effective way of making sure that the man you're looking for delivers himself into your hands without the need for yet another carefully-planned operation; and one wonders whether the police might not have arrested the editor's sister, or even one of his children, had his wife not been available. After all, once the principle of guilt by association has been established as an instrument of official terror, it's only logical that the net be extended as wide as is considered necessary by those who take the law into their own hands. The point is that the editor, Paxton Olu-Idowu (and never mind his wife), *had not broken any known law.*

It ought to be said that the police action in this particular case constituted an entirely new development in the ongoing war between government and journalists. 'Nigeria is not some banana republic where any madman can come and do what he likes,' was one editor's furious remark; and the union itself was quick to issue a statement, widely quoted in the press, which accurately reflected the public outrage at the police action:

The Nigerian Union of Journalists has described as most inhuman the arrest and subsequent detention of Mrs Paxton Olu-Idowu, wife of the editor of Republic Newspapers . . .

The Union, in a statement signed by its Secretary, Mr Jola Ogunlisi, deplored in the strongest terms the fresh attempt by police to harass law-abiding citizens and innocent dependants or families of journalists for any offence that might be perceived to have been committed by them.

Justifying its stand, the Union argued that there was nowhere in the world, including apartheid South Africa, where innocent dependants of journalists are hounded into detention in place of their journalist spouses.

National Concord, 21 June 1989

The Nigerian press – or at least the independent section of it – has a well-deserved reputation for being amongst the freest and most outspoken anywhere, and so it is. 'Ordeal of an Editor's wife' was the headline in another newspaper a fortnight after the event:

> For Mrs Florence Idowu the incident still seems like a nightmare. Two weeks after the horrifying incident that occurred when she was arrested in place of her husband . . . (she) still has a shaky and unbelievable tone in her voice and a rather bewildered look in her little eyes.
>
> As she narrates the story which probably has been told over and over again in the past two weeks, Florence Idowu, five months pregnant and in pain from the horrifying ordeal, looked straight, her eyes fixed on the wall in her cosy living room . . .
>
> *The Guardian*, 5 July 1989

And as if to leave the authorities in no doubt just where the battle lines had been drawn, the same edition of the newspaper carried a full-page article examining the human rights record of the regime, as well as an article on the notorious State Security (Detention of Persons) Decree Number Two of 1984, which allows for indefinite detention, without charge or trial, on the grounds of that convenient and by now thoroughly discredited catch-all, National Security.

Both these articles – 'Breaking the voices of dissent'; 'On the trail of Decree Two's monstrosity' – use the continued existence of Decree Two, and the increasingly liberal application of it against radicals and extremists and unpatriotic elements, as proof of the government's bad faith: it was Babangida's declared commitment to human rights which he used as the moral justification for seizing power in his maiden broadcast to the nation on the day of his coup in August, 1985:

> We recognise that a government, be it civilian or military, needs the consent of the people to govern if it is to meet its objectives. We do not intend to rule by force . . . Fundamental rights and civil liberties will be respected.

Fine words, no doubt, although there is something chilling in the formulation. 'We do not intend to rule by force' might contain the unspoken, 'but we will if we have to'. And since the police in a military State do not go around breaking up conferences and arresting journalists' wives without instruction from the military itself, one must assume that the President's patience had finally run out, and that the commitment to respect civil liberties was just so much rhetoric. In the words of Dr Tunji Abayomi, president of the Trial Lawyers Association of Nigeria, 'Respect for the fundamental human rights of Nigerians is not any different now from what it was under the previous governments. It is not better or worse, short of a proclaimed commitment to the preservation of the human rights of Nigerians'.

That is to say, the government was now seen to have itself abrogated its authority to govern by undermining – if not repudiating – the moral basis on which it seized power in the first place. As such, it could no longer count on the allegiance of the governed. It remained in power only through the rule of force, for which it relied on a battery of decrees with which to intimidate the growing opposition. Decree Two might be the most obnoxious of them, but it was not the only one which was causing concern. The Civil Liberties Organisation (CLO), in their Annual Report for 1988, *Violations of Human Rights in Nigeria*, catalogued seven separate decrees which precluded courts 'from enquiring into whether or not any of the constitutional guarantees of fundamental rights are complied with by the decrees or the tribunals acting under the decrees'. These include the Constitution (Suspension and Modification) Decree Number One of 1984, which suspended certain parts of the 1979 constitution providing for the prompt trial of suspects; the Robbery and Firearms Decree Number Five of 1984, which provided for the death sentence by a Military Tribunal on conviction of armed robbery, without the possibility of appeal; and the Public Officers (Special Provisions) Decree Number Seventeen of 1984, which empowered 'a government authority

49

or department to dismiss, remove or compulsorily retire any public officer for any reason ranging from ill-health, age, corruption, or "public interest", and such action cannot be challenged in any court whatsoever'.

The existence of the CLO, founded by two young lawyers, Olisa Agbakoba and Clement Nwankwo in October, 1987, provides an insight into the growing consciousness on the part of Nigerians that respect for fundamental human rights is an absolute pre-requisite of any civilised nation; as Olisa Agbakoba put it in his introduction to the Annual Report: 'Surely the ideal of a peaceful, happy nation can only be built on the foundation of a just and free society.' It is important in this context that the CLO is only one of a number of similar organisations dedicated to this ideal. Mention has already been made of the Trial Lawyers Association of Nigeria; while I was in the country Dr Beko Ransome-Kuti, the brother of the musician, Fela Aniku-lapo-Kuti, announced the formation of a Committee for the Defence of Human Rights following the arrest and detention of Chief Gani Fawehinmi for his part in the anti-SAP conference. Significantly, Dr Ransome-Kuti singled out Decree Two for special mention on the grounds that it constituted 'a gross infringement on the fundamental rights of Nigerians'.

I should add that the increasing number of such organisations can't yet be said to represent the dominant ethos in the society. I still came across any number of middle-class professionals who insisted that the issue of human rights was a fanciful abstraction unsuited to the Nigerian 'reality'. The reason for this is complex and has a lot to do with negative responses to cultural values which would take a separate essay to unravel. For the present, it is enough to say that groups like the CLO operate in isolation from the very people who could – and should – have afforded them protection, which was why Clement could be set upon by fifteen thugs as he was preparing to travel to New York in February this year on CLO business. It's possible that the timing of his beating was entirely fortuitous, and that his assailants were unconnected with those in power who wanted to teach him a lesson; but the authorities would then have to explain why only his passport was stolen, and why he had so much trouble obtaining a replacement.

Much the same had happened to Festus Iyayi. He was picked up last year and detained for a month under Decree Two because of his activities as president of the Academic Staff Union of Universities (ASUU); more specifically, for a strike he organised against the government's policies: 'ASUU understood that it had to take on the national economic problems because our destinies in the universities is tied to the destiny of the country as a whole. ASUU was, and is, a patriotic organisation. The leadership of the union was concerned about the future of the country,' he told me when I interviewed him in London shortly after his release. He also described how he was stripped to his pants and put in a cell with ordinary criminals who were ordered to beat him up.

When he was finally released he discovered that he had been 'retired' from his teaching post at the University of Benin, courtesy of Decree Seventeen, and that his wife and children had been thrown out of their university accommodation. By a stroke of good fortune Festus went on to win the Commonwealth prose prize for his third novel, *Heroes*, within weeks of his release, but it's doubtful whether the government was in any way embarrassed by the attendant publicity. He was only a writer, after all; he had only written a book which nobody would conceivably read – nobody that mattered, that is.

Achievement in Nigeria is always an individual affair. Worse yet, that achievement is only ever realised *against* a political system which hasn't fundamentally changed in thirty years. Nigerians can win all the Nobel prizes in the world and it won't make the slightest difference to the daily lives of Nigerians. And yet it is only nations which are able to harness the energy and the talent in the society that can put satellites into space and cure tropical diseases. Unfortunately, Nigerian governments can think of nothing better to do than beat up writers and arrest pregnant women.

2

'Those riots were nothing. They were just testing the soldiers, that's all. Next time . . .' He shook his head and laughed. I was on the last leg of the journey back from Enugu, where I had left Peter battling with the telephone and suspected malaria. It was dark as we pulled out of Benin motor park. The expressway was empty of traffic for long stretches at a time, and as we sped through the night my fellow passenger regaled me with stories about police complicity in armed robbery. One senior officer was even said to keep the corpses for a day or two in the boot of his car, which he would then park outside his favourite drinking parlour and invite people to take a look.

The stories weren't meant to frighten but, in a way, to reassure, which was why strict and literal truthfulness was irrelevant. By telling these stories my companion was imaginatively re-creating the terror he thereby hoped to avoid. It was a form of sympathetic magic. The Benin-Lagos expressway is amongst the most dangerous in the country, so much so that when we stopped to pick up a lone figure who loomed out of the surrounding darkness the driver insisted on frisking him before he allowed him to enter. The man himself understood our fears and readily submitted to the body search. The usual practice of armed robbers was to murder their victims since they themselves faced mandatory execution, without appeal, if caught and convicted. Such are the levels of insecurity under which Nigerians are daily forced to live, which is why the society is so volatile. It didn't need the present economic hardship to cause the explosion in May, but combined with the insecurity it was perhaps inevitable.

By all accounts the government was badly shaken by the scale of the riots. 'We can't allow the civilians to disgrace us out of office,' the President said in an address to the armed forces immediately afterwards, a sentiment which was apparently endorsed in even more trenchant tones in a recent issue of the Army's in-house journal, *SOJA*. Such a sentiment, openly stated, was immediately construed by the civilians as a declaration of war, which is what it was, and for the first time in post-Independence Nigerian history the military had publicly acknowledged itself to be a deliberate instrument of internal control. In terms of the eventual emergence of democracy in Nigeria this new perception of the armed forces might be just as well, but the danger in the short-term was that the army, having lifted all self-restraint, would then proceed to act with the shameless brutality of an occupying force. And it was in precisely these terms that people interpreted the government's handling of the anti-SAP conference; in Soyinka's words:

> Long before the public eruption on campuses and on the streets, the nation was already markedly up in protest. Now, after the riots, the military appears to have risen in protest, and is manifesting its own form of violence on the people by acting to frustrate the exercise of their fundamental rights as was amply demonstrated at the aborted 'Alternative to SAP dialogue'. The arrest and detention of the wife of a wanted journalist, this uncivilised taking of a hostage by the state is yet another notch in this damn-it-all engagement of the reverse gear in the military's civic responsiveness. The military has now lapsed several stages, and deliberately so, even from its halting reduction of its social alienation. This is the stark truth, and its definition is one of retrogression and a lack of maturity.
>
> *The Guardian*, 6 July 1989

I very much regretted missing the anti-SAP conference, but Festus told me what happened when I finally caught up with him. He said: 'Adewale, I wish you had been there that day. You would have seen with your own eyes what is going on in this country. They were determined from the start that we would not hold the conference. First they barred us from entering the hall we had rented from the Nigerian Labour Congress, so we walked over to Gani's compound, which was nearby. They followed us there and refused to let us assemble. Gani then said we should go into his chambers. Again, they wouldn't leave us alone. We moved upstairs to his sitting room for some refreshments and they came and said, "Don't talk, don't talk". So we just sat there. They didn't like that. They grabbed Gani and Tai Solarin and Imoudu and took them away.'

Festus spread his hands out before him, surprised perhaps that he was still at large, that he hadn't been arrested along with the others; then he shrugged and said: 'Can you imagine? We were sitting down in somebody's private residence and yet they followed us inside and refused to let us discuss privately amongst ourselves. If they had been able to they would even have stopped us thinking. This is a fascist government. It's only a matter of time before they come looking for me.'

Both Tai Solarin and Michael Imoudu were released that same evening. Gani Fawehinmi is still in custody under Decree Two. According to press reports, he was flown to 'an unknown destination' in a military transport aircraft within days of his arrest. His family was told, after repeated enquiries, that he would be released only when 'the Federal Government is satisfied with the explanation of his role in last Saturday's anti-SAP meeting'.

For a while it looked as if the government had overstepped the mark and that there would be a fresh explosion of popular discontent. Overnight, posters of Gani appeared on walls and billboards all over Lagos with the legend: IBB, Where is Gani?; Free Gani Now!; and several newspaper editorials were quick to point out that it was the government itself which had challenged those who disagreed with its economic policies to produce an alternative. Gani was the people's lawyer, the man who took on government without regard for his own safety, a brave man and a maverick, like Fela Kuti.

Gani has himself repeatedly claimed that the government is determined to 'eliminate' him, a claim which is amply corroborated by his own experiences at the hands of the police, most notably in connection with his prosecution of the two security officers he alleges are responsible for the murder of Dele Giwa, the editor of *Newswatch* magazine who was killed by a parcel bomb in October, 1986. Last March, for instance, he was attacked outside the law courts by an assailant who was heard to shout, 'For years you have been abusing the president. We know you're planning a coup. We will deal with you. We will kill you.' Gani was subsequently charged with breach of the peace and detained overnight without the option of bail. Now he had been flown to a secret place. Why? What did they want to do with him that they had to sneak him away under cover of darkness?

'This is a fascist government,' Festus had said. I'm usually wary of the way 'fascism' is loosely used as a synonym for authoritarianism, but in the context of the government's own actions it seemed an entirely appropriate description of what they were doing. And then, with perfect timing, the government gave added substance to Festus' charge by arbitrarily closing down six of the country's universities for an entire academic session:

The Armed Forces Ruling Council (AFRC) yesterday ordered that the Universities of Lagos, Ibadan, Benin, and state universities of Bendel, Imo and Lagos should remain shut until March 31, 1990.

Education Minister, Professor Jubril Aminu, who announced the AFRC's decision at the end of its one-day meeting in Lagos, also announced September 30, 1989 as the re-opening date for both campuses of the University of Nigeria (Nsukka) and the Ondo State University.

The Federal Government Colleges at Enugu and Okigwe are to remain closed indefinitely until the Federal Ministry of Education ordered their re-opening . . .

Professor Aminu said these institutions could only be re-opened if their authorities, and the state in which they were located, were satisfied that peace and order would be maintained.

According to him, the students would have to sign an undertaking to be of good behaviour for the rest of their stay and to pay reparation charges as may be levied by the appropriate authorities.

The Punch 27 June 1989

This was the students' 'punishment' for the part they played in the May riots, but all it really demonstrated was the wanton viciousness of a regime which also punished the lecturers for their 'apathy' during the demonstrations by announcing that they wouldn't be paid their salaries for the duration of the closures. Student representatives subsequently took the government to court to challenge the legality of the closures, but the government had itself already 'legalised' its options in the form of Decree Sixteen of 1985 which transferred the traditional function of university senates to a government body, the Nigerian Universities Council (NUC).

Universities, of course, are always the primary target of official repression, not only because they generate the ideas which will certainly prove fatal to illegitimate regimes; but because, in a country as diverse, as disorganised and as fragmented as Nigeria, the universities share one important feature in common with the military itself: the ability to operate politically at a national level. This is why Decree Sixteen specifically forbids the use of university auditoria for political meetings, as defined by the NUC-appointed Vice-Chancellor of the university concerned. It also explains why members of staff identified as radicals have been 'retired' in increasing numbers under Decree Seventeen:

In a bid to enforce its May 11 order on university teachers to steer clear of Third Republic politics, government will soon start forcing out disobedient teachers from the various university campuses. Vice Chancellors have been asked to compile a list of their teachers covertly involved in partisan politics. Affected persons would subsequently be sacked . . .

The Guardian, 18 June 1989

The most recent 'retirement' was that of Dr Bala Usman, one of the country's foremost historians, who subsequently pointed out in a newspaper interview that the government hadn't even offered a definition of what constituted 'politics' in the first place:

> You may think it means you can express an opinion, but how do you know? Already in Cross River State they are saying that if you don't believe in SAP you should resign from the government, as if the government belongs to them. The government of Nigeria is not the property of these people. I have told these military people this many times. And it is necessary for Nigerians to tell them. They don't have that right.
>
> *The Guardian*, 24 June 1989

But the government knows that definitions might be dangerous. As of now, elections are promised for the Third Republic in 1992. Only two political parties will be allowed to contest the elections. Both parties are to be chosen by the military; worse yet, the military has already ruled out 'extremists' as undesirable. Who is an extremist? They're not saying, but everyone knows that it's a euphemism for anybody they consider unreliable; anybody that is, who offers a genuine vision of a more equitable society. They can't admit this, of course, since to do so would finally dispel any lingering notion that they were serious about the transition to democratic rule.

Democracy is not the name of the game and it never has been, but the military knows perfectly well that it is only tolerated in power when it poses as a caretaker government. This then gives them the necessary breathing space to concentrate on more important matters, for instance helping themselves to a share of the country's wealth. Unfortunately for the Babangida administration, thirty years of corrupt leadership has taxed the credulity of even the most optimistic Nigerian citizen, hence the need for ever more stringent decrees with which to legitimise what can only be described as a species of armed robbery. Any genuinely patriotic government would soon uncover irregularities concerning foreign loans and Swiss bank accounts, in which case the present leadership would be lined up against the wall and shot – under Decree Five.

Everybody knows that Nigeria is not going to suddenly become a democratic nation in 1992. This includes the foreign lenders who want to ensure that the economic policies which are presently contributing to growing illiteracy rates, rising infant mortality and levels of desperation on the streets of all the cities – 'Master, won't you help me?' – can't be sabotaged by a bunch of socialists who imagine there is an alternative to the new imperialism. One doesn't have to be an economist (or even a radical) to see that there is precious little industry in Nigeria to structurally adjust, no British Steel or Ford Motor Company or ICI that needs to be streamlined for the twenty-first century. And the few industries that do exist, small concerns all of them, are busy going to the wall because they can no longer afford to buy the dollars to buy the raw materials that they need to survive, let alone compete with the flood of imports from economies which can properly be said to be structurally adjusted.

It is easy to see why certain nations are keen on encouraging – or imposing – rigid economic policies on certain other nations, and why they are prepared to reward their 'Third World' partners with ever more loans to ensure that those nations will never be able to repay. The whole point of the exercise is to turn Nigerians into bonded labourers, which is only one step above slavery.

Still, I had to admire the audacity of the Nigerian leaders who readily collude in the denigration of their own country. Less than a week after the report in *The Republic* which had led to the imprisonment of the editor's wife, the following appeared on the front page of another newspaper:

AIKHOMU HAS BEEN CLEARED

The presidency yesterday reacted for the first time to allegations of official impropriety made by a detained businessman . . . against the Chief of General Staff, Vice Admiral Augustus Aikhomu.

According to a NAN (News Agency of Nigeria) report, the press secretary to the Chief of General Staff, Malam Yusufu Mamman, told the state house correspondents that the police had investigated the allegations and found that there was no 'iota of truth in them'.

He said that the lawyers who went to court to seek an injunction for an order compelling the Inspector General of Police to investigate the allegations were only being 'uncharitable and mischievous'.

Vanguard, 23 June 1989

It might have been more honourable for Aikhomu, or indeed his press secretary, to spit in the faces of the assembled journalists, but then Nigerians know how much their rulers despise them that they can feed them nonsense of this sort; and it was a student leader who told me about the half-hour television documentary of the President's children at the annual games in their Swiss boarding school, the same children who are apparently flown home every weekend in one of the seven presidential aircraft. Don't even talk about patriotism in the Nigerian leadership. They know very well that Nigeria has no future, since they are the ones busy wrecking it. That is why it means nothing to them to close down a few universities, which in any case their own children will certainly not be attending.

'We have to drag these people out of office,' the student said, re-echoing the sentiments I had heard on my previous trip twelve months before; 'if necessary, we must be prepared to die in the process.' It's easy – and comforting – to dismiss this kind of talk as hot-headed idealism, but the passion and commitment that impressed me again and again in all the students I met mocked any suggestion that they could be patronised. They understood only too well that their own future had already been mortgaged, and that the longer they delayed the less likely were their visible chances of survival. In other words, they had nothing to lose.

ARISE IN DEFENCE OF OUR COUNTRY!
Great Nigerian Students,

Today the fate of our country is in the balance. With widespread unemployment, cuts in spending on public services with the concomitant effects of commercialised education, health services and transportation, and the regime's firm commitment to International Finance Capital, the stage is being set for the total enslavement of our people and unmitigated disaster for our country.

The debt burden on the neck of every Nigerian including those in the womb has been conservatively put at N4,000.00.* In fact mortality has dramatically increased because of malnutrition, disease and the increasingly inaccessible health services. The hospitals are without drugs, water and regular electricity supply with the doctors fleeing to Saudi Arabia and Europe. Drugs have become so expensive, sometimes costing more than the average salary of a Nigerian worker. Per capita income of workers has declined to N10.75 per month in real terms.

Education has sharply declined, with enrolment into Primary, Secondary and Tertiary institutions of learning decreasing every year. Aspiring young Nigerians into higher institutions and with the energetic pursuit of government policy of rationalisation which has led to the closure of faculties, departments and outright phasing out of some schools. Students study under impossible conditions of hunger, dilapidated structures, empty laboratories and unaffordable cost of books.

While we are groaning and moaning every day under the crushing weight of neo-colonial stranglehold, our ruling class is continuing to launch plans that will make life more unlivable for us. With the strategic oil sector of our economy firmly in the hands of imperialists, the government is concluding plans to sell the little we have left to foreign interests. Public corporations and assets like the Nigeria Airways, Nigeria Airports Authority, Nigeria National Shipping Line, Nigeria Electric Power Authority, the Banks and Insurance Companies etc, etc are under threat of being disposed of to foreign and local looters under the beautiful names of privatisation, commercialisation and debt-equity swap . . .

Nigerian students cannot afford to watch any longer while

their lives are being battered. We have appealed and demanded. They have refused to budge. We have been patient enough. NO TO IMPERIALISM! NO TO THE IMF/ WORLD BANK! YES TO A GREATER NIGERIA! LONG LIVE NANS!

This was the statement issued by the National Association of Nigerian Students (NANS) prior to the May demonstrations. Apart from anything else, it is a statement of great patriotism. Only those who believe in their own potential greatness are able to generate such levels of anger. I don't doubt that Nigeria has a future, but just how many will be sacrificed in the process of realising it is a question that can only be answered by those who have determined the exact number of people they will imprison and shoot . . . for what? A standard of living? The exercise of power for its own sake? Alas, yes, and yet they have the temerity to talk of conferring human rights on those same people they incarcerate and kill.

'. . . there was not an atom of foresight or of serious intention in the whole batch of them, and they did not seem aware these things are wanted for the work of the world,' Conrad wrote in another context, but he might as well have been referring to the present Nigerian leadership. This leadership won't listen, of course, but will insist instead on construing everything that I've written as unpatriotic and extremist. So much the worse for them. Nigeria is too big and too vibrant to be held to ransom by a government which daily demonstrates its own lack of patriotism with such open contempt. But how does one tell them that their nemesis will be at hand when there are no more anti-SAP conferences to break up; when, in short, people are no longer interested in talking? By then it will be too late.

June 1989

*£1.00 = N11.60 (Exchange rate as in 1989)

The satanic forces

As a state instrument of internal control, and even in the conduct of foreign policies (including terrorism), it is possible to suggest that religious fanaticism has once again attained prime position as the most implacable enemy of the basic rights of humanity.

Wole Soyinka: *Religion and human rights*

Following the outbreak of the Rushdie affair Wole Soyinka, the Nigerian dramatist and Nobel laureate, issued a characteristically combative statement calling on writers around the world to bombard Iran with pastiches of *The Satanic Verses*; and added: 'If Salman Rushdie is unnaturally and prematurely silenced, the creative world will launch its own *jihad*.' According to unconfirmed reports Soyinka himself received a death sentence within twenty-four hours of his statement. The arrow of (divine) retribution in this instance was said to have been fired, not from Tehran, but from the ancient Islamic city of Kano in northern Nigeria.

Of Nigeria's estimated one hundred million people – one quarter of the continent's entire population – roughly half are Moslems. From the point of view of the Islamic world, this number alone makes it easily the most important country in sub-Saharan Africa: an Islamic Republic of Nigeria would effectively ensure the Moslem domination of the West African sub-region. It was the direct result of Arab pressure which led the government of President Ibrahim Babangida, himself a Moslem, to secretly join the Organisation of Islamic Conferences (OIC) in January, 1986. When the news leaked, as it always does in Nigeria, the ensuing sectarian violence forced the government to withdraw.

At the moment, the Constituent Assembly in the Federal Capital of Abuja (as distinct from the administrative capital of Lagos) is debating the constitution for the Third Republic in 1992, the year in which the military has promised to return power to an elected civilian government. The final draft of the constitution, which seeks to remedy the faults in the 1979 constitution that ended with the downfall of the Second Republic in 1984, is already overdue. The delay is caused by the Moslem delegates to the Assembly, who want to extend the provisions for *shari'a* courts in certain civil cases already guaranteed in the suspended constitution. To the non-Moslems, particuarly the Christians, this is a clear case of give them an inch and they take the whole country; and it was only last year that the Catholic Archbishop of Lagos, Dr Olubumni Okogie, accused the government of planning to turn Abuja into an emirate: 'When the government gives its approval to construction plans of public places and ministry gates bearing Islamic crescent and arrow insignia instead of the Federal Government's shield, is there any doubt that it is turning Abuja into an Islamic capital of an Islamic state?'

This is not hysteria on the Archbishop's part. The quest for an Islamic Nigeria predates even the formation of Nigeria as a unified country by the British authorities in 1919. The *jihad* of *Usumanu dan Fodio* in the early nineteenth century was fired by the dream to 'dip the Holy Book in the Sea'; and although he was halted well before he reached the Atlantic, large parts of Yorubaland in the south-west of the country were subjugated by his troops. The mass conversions to Islam are seen today in the number of 'southerners' who make the annual pilgrimage to Mecca.

In the meantime, Islamic fundamentalism continues to pose the most serious threat to the country's fragile stability. Only recently, a Moslem leader, Sheik Abubakar Gumi, warned that Nigeria would disintegrate along religious lines if a Christian emerged as President of the Third Republic. That he wasn't immediately imprisoned under the notorious Decree Two was interpreted in many quarters as official sympathy for the sentiment expressed. There has been no shortage of writers, journalists, trade union leaders and human rights activists incarcerated over the last two years for their supposed threat to national security.

On the other hand, the government may be frightened of the possible consequences of imprisoning such a prominent Islamic figure. Anyone who doubts the fanaticism of Nigerian fundamentalists need only consider the scale of religious disturbances over the last decade which have rendered large areas of the north ungovernable. The most chilling explosion occurred in Kano in December, 1980, under the direction of an itinerant Islamic preacher known as Maitatsine. According to the official *Report of Tribunal of Inquiry on Kano Disturbances (1981)*, the city was brought to a standstill for three weeks. It took a military operation to restore order. By then four thousand people were dead. Maitatsine was himself killed in the course of the fighting, but his followers continue to turn up at irregular intervals all over the north. They believe, as do many Moslems, that if they die as martyrs they will go straight to paradise. For this reason they engage even armed units of the mobile police, themselves notorious for their barbarity against protesting students and striking workers.

It is against this background that one has to understand the position in which Soyinka now finds himself, but which he will already have anticipated. The quote this article opens with is taken from a speech he delivered at a conference in Paris in January last year, in the course of which he identified 'variants of (the) extremist virus' in his own country, and called upon the United Nations to declare the 1990s the 'Decade for Secular

Options' as part of a worldwide strategy for dealing with the fundamentalist threat:

> What response . . . can we offer when . . . horrifying events are sanctioned and promoted by a corporate existence which we call a state, when mass executions are routine, for no other cause than the courage of the victims which nerve them to resist state demands that they renounce their faith? A state where women are publicly lashed and even stoned to death for their refusal to submit to the jealously guarded dictatorship of male priesthood in matters of dressing or appearance? Where criminals, dissidents, adherents of dissenting faiths and economic saboteurs are lumped together under convenient titles as 'agents of Satan on earth', 'enemies of the Living Faith' and other versions of religious rhetoric which then become their own authority for their consequent imprisonment, torture and dehumanisation?

To the European, of course, all this might sound excessive, but the European world is only indirectly threatened by the ideological battle of the Word: Mohammed against Rushdie; *The Koran* against *The Satanic Verses*; fanaticism against the secular ideal. There can be no compromise between the two. Only a secular society has the capacity to generate the levels of internal criticism and debate – primarily through literature – which is the difference between stagnation and progress. The outcome of this battle will determine whether Nigeria develops its undeniable potential to become a force on the world stage, or whether it degenerates into another Sudan where the parliament argues the merits of cross-limb amputation as the Nile floods the city and tens of thousands of the country's citizens (but only infidels, after all) die of starvation in the war zone. After three decades of independence Africa has reached breaking-point; and it may be just as well that fundamentalist Islam in sub-Saharan Africa's most important country is forcing us to choose the kind of society we want in the twenty first century.

Supping with the devil

A few months ago I asked the Chairman of the South African Publications Appeal Board, Professor JCW van Rooyen, whether he would consider writing an article for us. I didn't expect a reply. I wrote with the same sense of impotent rage with which I had once phoned the South African Embassy in London to yell at some minion after I had read a newspaper report about a fourteen-year-old girl, Happy Cleopatra, who had been held in detention for three months without charge or trial under Section Twenty-Nine of the Internal Security Act of 1982.

Behind my rage, the superficial need to hurt – and superficial because quickly satisfied in the case of the Embassy official who obligingly lost his temper – I was distracted by the transcripts I had before me of the Appeal Board decisions on a wide range of material from girlie magazines to political tracts to serious novels to 'educational' videos; and what disturbed me about them wasn't only that the sophistication of the judgments made it impossible to dismiss the censors as philistines and have done with it, but that these particular censors participated at an official level in a political system which was literally inhuman.

The failure was on my side. I shouldn't have allowed myself to imagine that government censors were, by that fact alone, intellectually backward, however seductive – and comforting – such a view might be in the South African context, and however neatly it might have mirrored the political reality of apartheid. And I knew already, from reading a few years ago the judgment on Solzhenitsyn's *The First Circle* by the Session of Soviet Writers' Secretariat, that one might have reservations about the apparatus of official censorship and yet be sympathetic to some of the literary judgments of the censors concerned. For instance, I agreed completely with the view that Solzhenitsyn's depiction of Stalin was 'pitifully naive and primitive', even if I thought the summary of the novel as 'anti-humanitarian' just plain silly.

Meanwhile, the case for South Africa is more problematical, if only because the ideological problems posed by the East-West divide are absent here. One's view of the Soviet Union – or the United States, for that matter – depends largely on one's political position; one's responses to South Africa are entirely moral. Apartheid is evil, period. There is no room here for euphemisms, and even less room for the semantics in which the Appeal Board itself deals, beginning with its own definition of censorship: 'The practice of excising parts of a book will only be resorted to when distributors offer to do so or accept it without opposition. To *oblige* distributors to excise parts of books would amount to censorship in the true sense of the word; a practice which runs contrary to the spirit of publications control in peace time.' But even to engage in abstruse intellectual debate, as one is tempted to do with the above, is an obscenity, and obscene in the face of that fourteen-year-old girl incarcerated for three months in order that a few are able to maintain a certain standard of living: swimming pools, motor cars, a houseful of servants to clean and cook, and wash your underwear. And, yet, what really sticks in the throat is that the South African censor can make literary judgments as subtle and as informed as that of any member of the Soviet Writers' Secretariat, even as the political system which they support, if only by default ('I'm just doing my job'), acts on the assumption that human beings can be discriminated against *in law*.

To begin with, it was disappointing to discover that one wasn't dealing with a bunch of rednecks who had minor fits every time the word 'sex' was mentioned; and disappointing because of the ease with which we have come to bracket a certain kind of sexual repression with the nastier forms of political reaction. The South African censor, it appeared, could even deal quite equitably with homosexual prostitution, as was the case in the film, *Christian F*, which was found to be 'not undesirable' and not even 'harmful to public morals', because the treatment of the chosen theme was unlikely to 'promote promiscuity or homosexuality.' Again, a book on female masturbation, *A Woman's Experience of Sex*, was allowed because, in the opinion of the censors, it was 'most imformative, is written in a sincere style and tends to be helpful in every respect of a woman's life'.

The censors were even capable of making the proper distinction between intention and result. To be sure, their obsession with 'prominent nipples' and 'exposed pubic hair' in a book of photographs taken on an Australian beach may sound a little absurd, but when they add that the reader of *Life's a Beach* is turned into 'a voyeur' because those photographed are obviously unaware of what is happening, one recognises that it is precisely the voyeuristic element, and the deeper corruption which this implies, that invests pornography with its peculiar nastiness. More importantly for our own purposes, the same judgment compares this book with another of its kind, *Bo* by John Derek, where the 'high artistic merit' of the photographs, nipples and pubic hair notwithstanding, is decisive in their final judgment.

And perhaps, when all is said and done, we may ourselves have become too inured to the sight of all those girlie magazines on the newsagents' shelves alongside *Yachting Monthly* or *Classic Motor Cars* as though there was no qualitative difference between them. I'm not at all convinced that I want my daughters to think of themselves as objects of the male fantasy every time they buy a packet of sweets; and I don't see how the continual reinforcement of such a demeaning and prurient image makes this society more 'liberal' or 'tolerant' than societies where such magazines are banned. The Appeal Board itself, in a separate ruling, is unhappy with any 'blatantly shameless (or disgusting) intrusion upon the privacy of the female form'; and it's at least arguable that even a relatively 'harmless' publication such as *Playboy* is just such a shameless intrusion. At any rate, we know that Hugh Hefner is not motivated by any higher ideal than to make money, the *raison d'etre* of the professional pornographer. I certainly wouldn't want to find myself in the position of defending his right to publish his magazine, and I just might be convinced by the argument to ban it.

That aside, the South African censor is not even disturbed by the treatment of 'sex across the colour line' – and how old-fashioned that sounds! – as in the case of the unbanning of another book, *Sexual Life Between Blacks and Whites*. In one's naivete this was perhaps the area where one might have reasonably anticipated a display of collective apoplexia by the Board members – good Afrikaaners, all of them: Mr J J H Malherbe (Acting Chairman), Rev P R van der Merwe; Prof C E Pretorius, Rev J J de Jager – instead of which we find unexpected praise for the book's 'sober, unemotional style' and its 'impeccable' language. But even more startling, it is in the course of the judgment on this book that one finds a corresponding sophistication in the treatment of politics. The original banning order had cited the appeal within the book 'to more and more liberation' as justification for its action; the board dismisses this argument by asking why such an appeal 'should be regarded as in any way morally reprehensible'.

This level of political sophistication is borne out in one judgment after another. An issue of *Pace* magazine, for instance, which deals satirically with a meeting between a former South African President, B J Vorster, and Steve Biko, the murdered Black Consciousness leader, is allowed on the grounds that 'biting and emotional language is a typical feature of South African political life and that sufficient latitude must be allowed for political debate, criticism, and pleas for change.' Elsewhere, in the course of their judgment on a record initially banned because the lyrics were regarded as subversive ('We will fight for the right to be free/We will build our own society'), is unbanned because, in their opinion, 'the security of the state is not so fragile that a cliché-ridden and trite song . . . is likely to cause the slightest ripple.'

The Board is right, of course: the lyrics *are* cliché-ridden and trite, and it *is* absurd to imagine that a person listening to them will thereby become predisposed to violence. And in allowing the record to be freely distributed the Board is itself playing a rather clever political game of its own, if only by refusing to take such material seriously. In the process, they neatly forestall a fruitless debate by disarming the opposition even before it can vent its scorn, as in the case of a Christopher Hope novel, *A Separate Development*, where they argue that 'to read incitement to disorder and subversion into all this is to bring a kind of seriousness into a reading of the novel that the novel itself does not warrant or to ascribe to it an effect that it simply does not achieve.'

Reading these transcripts I was reminded of a television interview I once saw with the sheriff of some backwoods town in the American South during the civil rights movement in the late 1950s and early 1960s. After the usual inarticulate grunts to which we had been subjected from all the other sheriffs of all the other Southern towns, we were suddenly confronted with a man who calmly explained how he had carefully studied the collected speeches of Mahatma Ghandi and Martin Luther King the better to deal with the new threat to the prevailing social order. And he did deal with them: his was the only town in which Luther King himself admitted defeat. 'Listen, son,' the same sheriff said to one 'boy' he had put behind bars, 'this is a question of mind over matter: I don't mind and you don't matter.' Indeed; nothing personal: he neither liked nor disliked blacks. He had a job to do, and he did it. Meanwhile, his colleagues elsewhere were beating people over the head and achieving the very end they were attempting to avert.

The sheriff's chilling mixture of pragmatism, cynicism and ruthless intelligence goes beyond the merely human; and in demanding the same combination of qualities – in effect, playing strictly by the letter – he also denies the very humanity on which the justice of one's cause ultimately rests. Martin Luther King could quote the words of the Founding Fathers until hell froze over and it would be as productive as telling Professor van Rooyen that apartheid was a sin.

What, in that case, was I to make of the reply to my letter, which I received two months later?

Dear Sir,

Thank you for your letter of 16 June 1988. I subscribe to the Index on Censorship and have found it very interesting to read. As a judicial officer, I cannot, however, contribute to it by way of an article.

Kind regards

Professor J C W van Rooyen.

It was nicely typed on official, pale blue paper with the legend 'Republic of South Africa' in Afrikaans and English on either side of the country's coat-of-arms. If my intention had been to rile him and make him feel uncomfortable – however fleetingly: even the smallest pang of doubt would have been enough – then clearly I had failed; and if the exaggerated respect of the 'Dear Sir' was not meant as a deliberate insult, then the courtesy with which he countered my own calculated insult ('Thank you for your letter . . .') was – to put it mildly – disconcerting.

I felt a little like Wole Soyinka, who stumbled by chance on Radio South Africa one evening and heard his name mentioned alongside that of other African – but not South African – writers: 'MISTER Lenrie Peters, MISTER Ngũgĩ wa Thiong'o, MISTER Wole Soyinka etc, etc. There is such a weight of protocol upon this ordinary trapping of formal egalitarian distance, such implicit rejection of any patronising familiarity . . .' Precisely; no mention of MISTER Alex La Guma, the 'coloured' novelist and short story writer, who died in exile in Cuba. Alex La Guma had effectively been rendered invisible – a clear enough case of mind over matter – just as the imprisonment of Happy Cleopatra was implicitly denied by the subtle judgments of the Censorship Board.

In fact, there is no possible response to Professor van Rooyen's letter, just as there can be no dialogue with the South African Publications Appeal Board this side of apartheid. The debate has been taken beyond what can be reasonably said. The South African censor is attempting to defend an immoral position in political terms. This is the unspeakable lie at the heart of the letter. Even to engage in the debate is to participate in the evil that one abhors.

The devil finds work

> . . . racism is evil – human damnation in the Old Testament sense, and no compromises, as well as sacrifices, should be too great in the fight against it.
>
> Nadine Gordimer: *Living in the Interregnum*

In a recent article for *The Times* of London, 'Black hopes undermined' (28 January 1989), Ian Curteis, the British playwright, takes issue with the way in which cricket, 'the most English of games' (fair play, etc), has been dragged into the arena of apartheid, and British players, free men after all ('we must be free or die', etc), are forbidden by the International Cricket Conference (ICC) from engaging in friendly combat with their South African counterparts. He quotes with approval Norris McWhirter, leader of the so-called Freedom Association, who called the ICC decision to impose sanctions, 'A crushing blow to cricketers' freedom of choice', and promptly (but unsuccessfully) took the matter to court. One might wonder why people like Ian Curteis and Norris McWhirter see fit only to raise the issue of freedom *selectively*, and in a sport at that, but it seems that freedom is divisible: denial of the vote is not to be measured on the same scale as denial of the right to make money in whatever way you can.

One has become more than a little tired of those who plead tolerance towards South Africa on the one hand but condone, if only by implication, the incarceration and murder of human

73

beings on the other. Ian Curteis, who once accepted a short-term contract to work for the South African Broadcasting Corporation (SABC), thinks it sufficient to point to tyranny elsewhere on the continent in order to put South Africa into some kind of 'context':

> If the object of sanctions, economic, cultural or sporting, is to bring pressure to bear on countries with bad human rights records, why is South Africa singled out for special punishment?

He might have gone on to fashion a more respectable argument by telling us all about the nastiness of Master-Sergeant Doe of Liberia, the self-proclaimed illiterate and suspected cannibal, or President-for-Life Dr Hastings Banda or Malawi ('The same feet that ran and chased the master out of our country/Now strut on the platforms in the thick boots left by master')*, but he chooses instead to clinch the matter by hiding behind the 'much-respected' (?) New York-based Freedom House, the organisation which publishes an annual survey of human rights abuses around the world:

> The current report lists fifty-three countries, all members of the United Nations, with a *worse* human rights record than South Africa; twenty-eight are independent African states.

Let it be said at once that Africans themselves are the first to castigate their own tyrannical rulers, and that African jails are full of poets and journalists – and human rights activists – who are paying a high price indeed for their refusal to accept the subversion of democracy in their respective countries. Africans are not blind to the faults of their societies, merely mistrustful of those who attempt to appropriate the moral high ground for purposes which are less disinterested – and certainly more political – than is otherwise pretended by those attempting to defend the indefensible. An American organisation is not, by that fact alone, automatically in possession of the wherewithal to draw up such league tables, and their claim to be somehow 'objective' in these matters is itself suspect: all propaganda is necessarily objective; the challenge is to make us believe it's also the truth.

But South Africa is different, and all the Liberias and Malawis in the world, no matter the levels of degradation, cannot alter that fact. This difference isn't one of degree but of kind: South Africa is the only country in the world which discriminates against its own citizens *in law*. This apparently simple fact seems to escape that country's apologists, who then plead mitigating circumstances on behalf of those who deny others the vote:

> Two things strike the visitor forcibly: how fundamental are the changes of the last few years, and how they have come about in spite of, not because of, sanctions.
>
> Anyone interested in South Africa knows about the changes: the abolition of the pass laws, of job reservation for whites . . . the abolition of the Mixed Marriages Act . . .

A revolution, no less; but I wasn't aware that the freedom to go where you want or marry whom you like or live where you choose were negotiable in the first place. In fact they aren't commodities that can be granted, only fundamental rights that can be denied. Merely to stop denying them is hardly cause for praise or celebration. Meanwhile, our observant tourist, contemplating the happy natives in their own setting ('the research trip that was part of the contract would enable me to tour the country . . . and see with my own eyes what so many people become incoherent with rage about'), conveniently forgets that the disenfranchisement of these natives, the denial of the most basic of all human rights, is not even a matter for discussion in what is laughably called the country's Parliament.

This is at the heart of any discussion about South Africa, and never mind whether black and white – and coloured and Chinese and Malay and 'other Asian' and Griqua – are now permitted to sleep with each other; but in evading the central issue and pretending that the abolition of the Mixed Marriage Act is some kind of progress for which we should be grateful, Ian Curteis suggests that universal standards are not to be applied to the different 'races'. If so, this would explain why he appears to have no problems sympathising with the apartheid mentality.

This mentality is presently overseeing the third successive State of Emergency in which children are daily imprisoned and tortured without charge or trial for their 'subversive activities'. Naturally, when the State begins to incarcerate children they also make sure that they do so under cover of darkness: Behold, I come as a thief in the night; and we can certainly take some comfort from the knowledge that those who perpetrate evil are well aware of their alliance with the Devil. South Africa currently operates the most repressive censorship laws of any country in the world (including the rest of Africa), but to read Ian Curteis you would never guess. Having determined what he's going to see – progress – he also determines what he isn't going to see – censorship:

> I watched SABT-tv in hotel rooms, seeing nothing to support the accusation that it was the government's poodle. Moreover, the SABC – modelled on the BBC – still clearly regards programmes as a means of communication, not as political powerblocks in their own right.
>
> I saw excellent documentaries and plays, some with mixed-colour casts, which we will never see in Britain. For two British unions exercise political censorship over South African television programmes, denying us the choice of seeing them . . .

The twist at the end, the move from the apparent liberalism of the SABC to the strong-arm tactics of the British Trade Unions, who turn out to be the real enemies of freedom, defeats its own purpose at the same time as it reveals the underlying dishonesty – or naivete – of Ian Curteis' argument. His self-imposed brief is to examine the behaviour of the government in a fascist state, not the behaviour of trade unions in a democracy; and in wilfully confusing the different categories he obscures the intentions of either body: the action of the British trade unions is, precisely, a protest against the very censorship with which Ian Curteis charges them.

What, then, is the background against which this liberal SABC operates? The full text of the South African censorship laws would – and does – fill an entire book, but an idea of their scope is revealing. The State of Emergency regulations (and leaving aside the Defence Act, the Police Act, the Prisons Act, the Internal Security Act and the Publications Act) prohibits reporters, photographers, cameramen and their assistants from being within sight of the following: an illegal gathering; a physical attack on a policeman, soldier or prison warder or on a family member of any such official or on his/her property; a riot or behaviour classified as public violence or intimidation; any action by police or soldiers to terminate any of the foregoing events or actions or to 'follow up' on them; any application of force by a policeman or soldier against persons he believes are endangering public safety and order; action by police and soldiers in which people are arrested on suspicion of committing 'unrest' or are being detained under the state of emergency.

That is to say, the forces of 'law' and 'order' (dubious concepts in an illegitimate State) are permitted to do what they like – invisibly. Peaceful demonstrators demanding their basic democratic rights can be bullied and beaten by legalised terrorists (let us call them by their proper name) and the SABC is forbidden *in law* from showing the bloody scenes on television screens. Children as young as eight are detained without charge or trial and journalists are forbidden *in law* from mentioning their names. Journalists can be placed under house arrest and their newspapers are forbidden *in law* from publishing what they write.

Consider, then, a recent article by Fabius Burger in the (Johannesburg) *Weekly Mail*, 'Sliced but the censors are happy' (27 January–2 February 1989):

> The SABC has announced a list of some 45 films for next month. That should be exciting, but it isn't. The films will probably be scrutinised, cut and sanitised until they're little more than pulp for kiddies.
>
> That's to be expected from an organisation whose in-house

censors . . . can spend several hours arguing whether to allow Eliza Doolittle to encourage her favourite horse to move its 'blooming arse' when *My Fair Lady* was shown on television . . .

The number of cuts in films passed for release has increased. Among recent films banned outright are *River's Edge*, a suburban drama about classmates who protect their teen-murderer friend; *Zoo . . . La Nuit* (Night Zoo), a French-Canadian film about an ex-hoodlum and his father; *Betty Blue*, about an obsessive love-relationship . . .

And so on. But the real question is: Why does Ian Curteis – and *The Times* – need to pretend that the difference between South Africa and the rest of the world is one of degree only? Obviously, if he can do this then he can dismiss the case for sanctions on the grounds of his own logic, ie, if South Africa, why not Liberia?, and plead for dialogue instead of sanctions:

South Africa's immediate future must lie in coalition and co-operation. It is fast emerging from its long nightmare and needs our help, not our hatred.

The answer lies in his refusal to consider that South Africa is indeed an anomaly. The real measure of the apartheid regime isn't with Malawi but with Nazi Germany, its spiritual precursor. Ian Curteis' inability to make this connection suggests that the unspeakable lie – colour – operates at the same level at which it was once possible to overlook the murder of Jews on the grounds that, after all, they were only Jews. In other words, to argue that South Africa is a country like any other country is to accept the language of apartheid itself.

This language rests on the assumption (or, better, the lunacy) that colour is a meaningful attribute of human beings, which in turn is a measure of their worth. Apartheid doesn't talk of people but of races. These races are different from each other in terms of colour and only colour, hence the necessity for a Race Classification Board:

The devil finds work

The Minister of Home Affairs, Stoffel Botha, disclosed in Parliament that last year more than 1,000 were reclassified from one race group to another.

Weekly Mail, 13–19 June 1986

Such an impoverished vision of humanity is exceeded only by the crudity of the scale used to measure this same humanity: white at the top; black at the bottom; everybody else in between. To be black, therefore, means that you don't count; or, more accurately, that you count for less than each successive group above you. This means, in practice, that whites make the laws, that Indians and coloureds are permitted to discuss some of them, and that blacks, for whom these laws are largely made, ought to be grateful when some of the more absurd of them – the Mixed Marriages Act, say – are repealed.

But the 'long nightmare' of South Africa – from which, incidentally, it is only now beginning to show some signs of emerging – is the nightmare of a wholly relative universe, so that the repeal of the Mixed Marriages Act can only be construed as progress in relative terms. The absolutes of good and evil no longer apply. In such a universe language itself must be corrupted: 'I look at the constellations in the sky at night and what are the words I see written there? South Africa for the Christians' (President P W Botha). This is why even the notion of dialogue is a nonsense. Language itself assumes absolutes. Words like democracy, justice, equality – to say nothing of law and order – are not relative to different societies but absolute to all societies. A society which considers them relative is using language in the same way that a lunatic might be said to use it: to describe a private universe in which words are privately defined.

To argue in favour of dialogue with South Africa is to participate in the corruption of language, which is why it is possible for Ian Curteis not only to compare the SABC with British trade unions, but to go on and make the extraordinary claim that the former is somehow more liberal that the latter. Such a comparison cannot even be made. And in the process he

79

overlooks the way in which he has allowed himself to be used for the propaganda purposes of the regime he seeks to defend. When the SABC invites British playwrights to work for them on short-term contracts they do so not because they're committed to good television but because they're committed to good public relations. The publication of Ian Curteis' article in *The Times* is proof of their success on this score. The argument against dialogue, of which sanctions is a small part, rests wholly on the refusal to grant the devil a voice. Ian Curteis might choose to call this censorship; if so, the devil will be happy to concur.

*From Frank Chipasula: *NIGHTWATCHER: Nightsong* (Peterborough: Paul Green, 1986).

The problem of seeing

We inhabit one world, a world whose very survival depends
more than ever on mutual understanding.

Draft Declaration, *Challenging the Censors: A World News
Media Action Conference*, London, 16–18 January 1987

In order to render large numbers of human beings invisible you
merely have to attach a convenient label to them and then
pretend that they all conform to it. It is part of the magic of words.
The phrase 'Third World', invented by the French to denote
those areas of the world which were part neither of the first world
of the developed Western democracies nor of the second world
of socialism, functions in just this way. One has only to say it to
forget that we are referring to the majority of the world's
inhabitants embracing a multiplicity of radically different cul-
tures and covering most of the earth's surface. What, for
instance, do Peru and Nigeria have in common? Or Bangladesh
and Mexico? Or India and Swaziland? Only this: that they do not
belong to the area of the world which has attached this label to
them. That is to say, they are defined wholly in terms of the
perceptions of others.

This was brought out most clearly in a speech delivered by
David Ottaway, foreign correspondent of the *Washington Post*, at
the recent world conference on censorship held in London: 'The
Many Ways of the Censor: Trials and Tribulations of Third
World Reporting'. Even before he was allowed to speak we were

81

left in no doubt as to his credentials, which included a string of higher degrees in Political Science from every American university that matters, to say nothing of the five years he had spent in Africa in the mid-1970s as an accredited journalist.

As a journalist, and therefore a man of words, there was nothing fortuitous in the way in which he chose to begin his talk. He didn't begin in Africa, as one might have expected, but in France during the time of the Algerian War of Independence in the late 1950s:

> To a young, naive American student like myself, abroad for the first time and with no idea of what censorship could mean, the experience of reading French newspapers and weeklies with blank spaces scattered throughout their pages was a real eye opener. I simply had no idea that a Western, civilised country like France would indulge in such heavy-handed tactics to suppress news that was not to its liking.

The ease with which he brackets together 'Western' and 'civilised' as though there was an obvious, logical connection between them is, of course, telling: such emotive use of language is part of the intellectual climate of the modern world in which sweeping statements can be made with impunity about human societies that have automatically been relegated – third world, third best, third rate – to the bottom of the pile.

From France in the 1950s we move to Kenya in the 1970s, where our foreign correspondent files a story calling President Kenyatta's wife a crook. He is immediately invited to leave. His response is altogether more laconic:

> That baptism by fire into the ways used by Third World leaders to keep their dirty linen from being washed in public was not altogether shocking or unexpected to me. Already I had incurred the wrath of the late Emperor Haile Selassie, in whose country I was taking up residence, by writing a story . . . about how the government was quietly exporting grain while the people were starving . . .

The problem of seeing

His comparative maturity, implicit in his reference to his earlier naivete, seems to suggest that he is not as shocked as he was in France only because he is now older, wiser and, presumably, altogether more cynical. But this is not so. In fact he sees a qualitative difference between censorship in France and censorship in the 'Third World', and refuses to acknowledge that the French government, no less than the Kenyan and Ethiopian governments, is just as anxious to hide its dirty linen from the public gaze. But then he has high expectations of the one – 'Western, civilised' – and no expectations of the other – non-Western, uncivilised.

Or am I reading too much into it? Am I guilty of 'Third World' paranoia, that disease which afflicts representatives of societies which have the temerity to resist the imposition of alien labels? Unfortunately for David Ottaway, he unwittingly betrays himself when he comes to consider the case of South Africa, a country he can hardly avoid in any discussion of censorship:

> Are our problems as foreign correspondents becoming quantitatively or qualitatively worse? Is it simply because a white government is involved, or because it is so blatant, or because there are dozens of our colleagues and employees affected . . .?

South Africa has long presented First World commentators on Africa with a problem. To any African the matter is quite simple: a minority tribe has hijacked power and is busy incarcerating children in order to maintain that power. The emergency regulations, and with it the strict censorship laws, are part and parcel of the mechanism by which an illegitimate government attempts to impose its will on the majority of the country's citizens through brute force. The fact that this minority is white is important only to the extent that the same minority insists on the primacy of colour as the yardstick by which we are to judge humanity. To say that the use of such a yardstick betrays an insanity which would be laughable if it weren't so tragic is only to state the obvious. Or so one would have thought. But it is

Ottaway himself who has raised the unspeakable lie – colour – and seen fit to agonise over it: 'Is it simply because a white government is involved?' he asks; to which we reply: Is it possible than an important part of Ottaway's perception of the 'Third World' is that it is non-white? Is he suggesting that there are certain ways of behaving which are no more than we should expect from blacks but which we find shocking in whites? Is a black tyrant the norm and a white one the exception?

If the charge of racism is too easy – and too imprecise – to lay against the door of certain foreign correspondents from the 'civilised' world, it is one, after all, to which they lay themselves wide open. When Ottaway goes on to complain of the shabby treatment he receives from African Heads of State he is, according to his own perceptions, understandably perplexed:

> One major problem for American correspondents is the near total ignorance of Third World leaders about how Western media works and how to use it for their own ends. While the correspondent may regard his or her request for an interview with a leader or top minister as a chance to air their views, they seem to look upon it as a huge favour which they are uncertain will be rewarded in any way.

On the contrary, 'Third World' leaders know exactly how the Western media works because it has been working on them for as long as they remember. They also know that it can never be used for their own ends, proof of which is provided by Mr Ottaway himself in the opening sentence of his speech:

> You may not believe it, and I find a certain sense of irony in it now, but my first exposure to censorship was not in the wilds of black Africa . . .

Why the qualification of Africa as 'black'? Does one speak of 'white' Europe? And why 'the wilds'? Is this a geographical description of the continent, or does he mean it in the sense of barbarians? Perhaps the truth is that it is these 'Third World' leaders who possess a much better understanding of that same media than all the First World journalists under the African sun. This is to say nothing of the arrogance which assumes that 'Third World' leaders want to use the Western media for any ends. They might just want to be left alone to get on with the job of nation-building, a task already made difficult by the machinations of the Western media and its negative assumptions.

There was a point in his speech when Mr Ottaway made the familiar noises about the way in which ideology makes censorship possible. No doubt it does, but it is a truth which can only carry weight if it springs from a genuine humility that you, too, may be just as blinded by your own ideology. In a cheap aside not included in his published transcript, Mr Ottaway 'shared with us' – American terminology – a recent experience he had in Nigeria. Confronted with the President's press secretary during a press conference at the President's official residence, he demanded to know why two American journalists hadn't yet been issued with visas two months after they had applied, even though both journalists had written sympathetically about the country in the past and were ready to do so again in the future. He omitted to mention the rather important fact that there is no censorship of the press in Nigeria*, a fact he surely knows, but left the less knowledgeable members of the audience to draw their own conclusions. And as if to reinforce the suspicion that the Nigerian authorities were behaving in the way all 'Third World' authorities can be expected to behave, he immediately went on to make some unflattering comments about Malawi, a country which everyone knows to be an authoritarian one-party state ruled since Independence by a neurotic. Ironically, less than a month after Mr Ottaway's sermon, the President of Nigeria opened a top-level seminar in the country on national communication policy with these words:

> . . . an informed public opinion coupled with an enlightened citizenry constitute an essential prerequisite for the attainment of a progressive and stable state. Such an informed and

enlightened populace could evolve more quickly through media unhindered in the performance of their duties.

West Africa, 9 February 1987

But as Mr Ottaway spoke I recalled a recent report about a Colombian journalist who was denied entry into the United States – the land of the free and the brave – because of her political opinions:

> The most flagrant example of the 1952 McCarran-Walter act in action was the arrest and deportation in New York of the distinguished Colombian journalist, Patricia Lara, in mid-October (1986). Even though she held a valid US visa, she was turned away by Immigration and Naturalisation Service (INS) officials on 12 October when she arrived on a flight from Bogota. Her name had been found in a 'look-out book' containing details of foreign nationals who are thought likely to engage in 'subversive, terrorist or anarchist' activities while in the United States . . .
>
> The Colombian reporter's offence was probably her outspoken criticism of US policy in Central America. She has been a frequent visitor to Managua and Havana . . .
>
> *Index on Censorship*, January 1987

Nor was she the only recent case of censorship blinded by ideology in the immensely desirable First World. A few weeks earlier, a correspondent for a Belgian Socialist newspaper was denied entry after INS officials found 'subversive' literature in his luggage. And that same October, yet another Colombian journalist, Olga Behar, was 'detained in Miami when she arrived on an Iberia flight from Madrid, en route to Mexico . . . Her name also appeared in a "look-out book".'

If any of this had happened in a 'Third World' country we wouldn't have heard the end of it; as it is, we have to put up with American correspondents charging governments before the case has been proved and conveniently overlooking the mess in their own backyard. What this betrays is the arrogant conviction that they alone possess a monopoly on moral values, an arrogance which quickly degenerates into a propaganda war that helps no-one's cause. It certainly doesn't help in the fight against censorship – the ostensible reason for David Ottaway's presence at that conference – which must be resisted wherever it occurs. Simply to lump together disparate peoples under a convenient label and then make sweeping generalisations about them on that basis alone is to participate in the very censorship you claim to abhor. By seeing only what you want to see, by blinding yourself with what is effectively an ideology, you render entire societies invisible and deny them a voice. If we really mean it when we claim to 'inhabit one world, a world whose very survival depends more than ever on mutual understanding,' then we had better begin by listening to what everyone has to say. Censorship is not a matter of geography or 'race' but of human societies caught in a particular moment in history. It is for us to understand the conditions that produce it, which is a pre-requisite for understanding how to combat it.

*Alas, this is no longer the case. A new Media Decree has since come into force in the country which enables the government to decide who is and isn't permitted to practise as a journalist.

Out of Europe

CALIBAN   . . . and I'll be wise hereafter,
And seek for grace. What a thrice-double ass
Was I, to take this drunkard for a god!
And worship this dull fool!

Shakespeare: The Tempest

To mark the fortieth anniversary of the United Nations Charter on Human Rights, BBC television recently broadcast a series of five-minute programmes to highlight the plight of prisoners of conscience around the world. Each case was introduced by a well-known British personality. One programme was devoted to Zwelakhe Sisulu, the 'black' South African editor of the 'alternative' *New Nation* newspaper, who was freed within days of the programme after he had been held for nearly two years under Section Twenty-Nine of the Internal Security Act. Under this Act the authorities, who were permitted to hold him in solitary confinement for as long as they pleased, were not obliged to charge him with any offence. We may presume that his 'crime' was to have given space within the pages of his newspaper to reports of brutality in the townships by the guardians of law and order, but truth is always the first victim of self-serving myths, in this case the myth of racial inferiority.

The programme on Sisulu was fronted by Max Hastings, editor of the (London) *Daily Telegraph*, who spoke movingly about Sisulu's career to date and his current health problems as a result of his detention. Sisulu, who has just turned thirty-eight, was reportedly suffering from extreme depression and a dangerous heart condition. It is a familiar story, of course, and not only in South Africa: a previous programme highlighted the case of two South Korean brothers who have been held illegally for more than twenty years for taking part in a peaceful demonstration while they were students at the university.

But I wondered, as I listened to Max Hastings reiterate yet another tale of State terror against one of its citizens, whether he himself made the connection between the case of the man he was talking about and the politics of his own newspaper. Bearing in mind that Sisulu is a black and an African (important attributes, whichever way you look at it), I have before me an article which appeared in the *Daily Telegraph* just six weeks before its editor appeared on our television screens. The article in question, 'Out of Africa' (22 October 1988), was in the nature of a farewell letter by the paper's outgoing correspondent, Jeremy Gavron, following a two-year stint.

'Out of Africa' tells an even more familiar story to anyone acquainted with European myths concerning the backwardness of the simple African: 'Africa is still young'; 'Africa is still the dark continent'; 'Africans think in terms of their village, their tribe: they are pre-political'. Once upon a time it was enough simply to make noises about kinky hair, flat noses and protruding lips; but perhaps the Holocaust in Central Europe has demanded a more circumspect language with which to defend the indefensible.

And it isn't such a great leap, after all, for our departing Africa expert to move from the pre-political African in the dark continent (or: the horror, the horror!), to the following:

Kenya's leader, Daniel arap Moi, has been criticised for his steady dismantling of the country's British-style government. He has made his party – the only legal party – more powerful than the elected members of parliament: he has almost completely eroded the independence of the legal system, and he has begun to replace the secret ballot with public queueing. Moi's new system could not work in Britain, but perhaps they are not such a bad thing in Africa. At least they are African.

The scale of the opposition to Moi's authoritarian rule would seem to contradict the easy complacency of this irresponsible statement; and in so far as tyranny can be said to work in Kenya it does so to the same degree that the reign of the colonels can be said to have worked in Greece: by terror. The objects of that terror in either case – the lawyers and the academics and the writers and the students and the trade unionists, to say nothing of their relatives and friends – are conveniently overlooked as we erect our fanciful theories concerning the world-view (or: village-view) of the primitive African.

Item: Gitobu Imanyara, editor of the *Nairobi Law Monthly*, appeared in court on charges of 'theft' and 'misuse of a publishing licence' after publishing articles dealing with political detention and trials;

Item: Mirugi Kariuki, arrested in December 1986, continues to be held without charge or trial under Public Security Regulations. No official reason has been given for his detention, but he is said to have been accused of links with the left-wing opposition group *Mwakenya*. Recent reports received by Amnesty International suggest that he has required medical attention as a result of torture;

Item: John Muugai, accused of links with *Mwakenya*, died in prison on 5 May. He is believed to have been seriously tortured. Members of his family were only able to identify him from a mark on his leg;

Item: Bedan Mbugua, editor of the monthly magazine *Beyond*, was jailed for nine months for criticising the absence of a secret ballot during the recent elections.

Item: Raila Odinga, son of the veteran politician and sometime Vice-President Oginga Odinga, was arrested in Nairobi on 30 August. He is held under the Public Security Regulations, which allow for indefinite detention without charge or trial. He was arrested apparently in an attempt to silence his father, whose well-known left-wing views have caused embarrassment to President Moi.

This is a small selection from newspaper cuttings over the last four months. In fact it would be quite possible to fill an entire issue of *Index on Censorship* with case histories of those Kenyans currently detained for their opposition to 'African' one-party rule. But for what purpose? Jeremy Gavron has not – literally – heard them:

> Africa itself has a little bit of Caliban in it. Europe taught Africa language and its profit is to know how to curse. It may take fifty years, or a hundred, or even two hundred; but, give Africa time, and one day it may even write poetry.

This is the ultimate censorship, that one doesn't hear Caliban's curses, at least not in the usual sense of taking seriously the words uttered from the lips of a monster: 'Thou poisonous slave, got by the devil himself'. One doesn't even have to concern oneself with Caliban's pain. And, like Caliban – who, incidentally, does speak poetry: 'Be not afeard – the isle is full of noises/Sounds and sweet airs, that give delight and hurt not' – one comes perilously close to saying that such pain as the African experiences, when measured in the scale of human worth (will we also talk of the descending scale of mulattos and quadroons and octoroons?), is of little account. You can throw them into prison, you can torture them, you can even kill them if you like, and European correspondents observing the nightmare from the safety of their five-star hotels in Nairobi will tell you that, on balance, it may even be a good thing.

I'm sure that President Moi, or President Botha for that matter, will be happy to endorse Jeremy Gavron's sentiments. 'You people don't understand Africa,' the South African Foreign Minister recently told a gathering of (largely critical) foreign correspondents in Johannesburg, but he obviously reads the wrong papers. We can tell him that there are newspapers which believe, as he does, that Africans are different; that they aren't like Europeans; that their thick skulls are protection enough from the blows that batter them into dull submission: 'For this, be sure, to-night thou shalt have cramps/Side-stitches that shall pen thy breath up – urchins/Shall, for that vast of night that they may work,/All exercise on thee: thou shalt be pinched/As thick as honeycomb, each pinch more stinging/Than bees had made 'em.'

Poor Africa: any foreigner can say what they please, but those who publish such nonsense as they utter will materialise on our television screens to tell us all about a courageous, articulate African journalist who was incarcerated for two years because a certain myth concerning his inferiority had been taken to its logical conclusion. And, yet, oddly enough, the South African authorities would indeed appear to know more about Africa that do irresponsible European journalists. Zwelakhe Sisulu, after all, may be free, but according to the terms of his release on 2 December, he is forbidden to leave home at night, he cannot venture beyond Johannesburg without police permission, he cannot give interviews, he cannot participate in any form of journalism, and he cannot meet more than ten people at a time. Presumably, these self-same authorities are frightened by what *he* might say about their own illegitimate rule. *I* say, 'Shege danduru waka,' which may or may not be a curse in an ancient and honourable African language; but which, if it is – 'Europe taught Africa language' – will hardly cause our intrepid journalist any offence. This is just as well.

Mastering reality:
the need for a new vision*

The mastering of reality and its transformation requires the liberation of the mind from the superstition of power, which cripples the will, obscures self-apprehension and facilitates surrender to the alienating processes ranged against every form of human productivity.

> Wole Soyinka: *The Critic and Society: Barthes,*
> *Leftocracy and other mythologies*

I would like to dedicate this paper to Jack Mapanje, the Malawian poet, who has now been held in detention, without charge or trial, for two years; and I would like to begin by quoting from a letter by Maina wa Kinyatti, the Kenyan historian, who recently completed a six-year prison sentence for possessing what the regime of President Moi insisted on calling 'subversive literature':

Monday! It was glorious. I walked out of prison with my shoulders unbent, with my head unbowed to face the rough future of humanity. With courage and pride I embraced the sunshine of freedom; I breathed the fresh air of freedom . . . but I am bitter because those long years of my imprisonment were the best years of my life, they were the best years of my intellectual development and they were taken away . . .

I spent the last year of my imprisonment in solitary confinement. I was in the cell twenty-three hours a day, fed half-cooked beans, maize meal full of worms and sand, unwashed yellow rotten vegetables. Between March and

August 1987 I was put together with lunatic prisoners. I suffered unbearable mental pains. But I remained strong throughout, they were not able to break me. The main reason they were not able to break me was the fact that I drew strength, endurance and courage from the international community, from many international friends – unknown and known – who dropped everything to fight for my release. My heart goes out to them all.

Receiving this letter was without doubt the most touching moment in my three years as Africa editor of *Index on Censorship* magazine. It confirmed for me that, even from the perspective of London, it was possible to do something for a political detainee as far away as Nairobi. But it didn't lessen my basic uneasiness, this business of monitoring events in Africa from an office in London. I might equally be in Paris or Lisbon and it would amount to the same thing: Africa as seen and reported from the vantage point of Europe. We all know why this is so, of course, but our knowledge of the historical imbalance doesn't make it any less invidious. The point is to change it. But how?

Consider the case of the Civil Liberties Organisation (CLO) in Nigeria, which was founded by two Lagos-based lawyers in October 1987. In December last year they published their first Annual Report, *Violations of Human Rights in Nigeria*, copies of which were sent to every member of the Armed Forces Ruling Council. They were promptly detained and questioned for several hours, and for a while it looked as if they were going to be charged with subversion.

One could perhaps say that the CLO didn't help its case by advertising, in such a public manner, violations of human rights by a government which had seized power on a pro-human rights platform; but then the point of the exercise was, precisely, to demonstrate to those same authorities that such abuses were unacceptable, and that it was their duty, as Nigerian citizens, to hold public officers accountable for their (extremely public) actions.

Compared to the rest of the continent, Nigeria (and Senegal, I might add) is a relatively 'liberal' society, a fact which can be gleaned from a glance at the country's notoriously volatile press. But if even the Nigerian authorities can make life difficult for those who choose to criticise what they do, what are we to say when we turn to Kenya, or Malawi, or the Congo, or Equatorial Guinea, or Liberia, or . . . ? But the list is a long one, as we all know, and it would include most of the countries on the continent.

As regards Malawi, for instance, Jack Mapanje was imprisoned without charge or trial because he was supposed to have said something to someone regarding somebody else while he was having a beer with colleagues in the university bar. I have this on hearsay only but, in the case of Malawi, rumour is our most reliable source of information, in itself a comment on the authoritarian nature of the regime. At any rate, we *do* know that he didn't accuse the police of shooting demonstrators with live ammunition; we *do* know that he didn't accuse the state security service of detaining people indefinitely; we *do* know that he didn't accuse soldiers of attacking innocent civilians and beating them to death. We know, in other words, that he didn't do what the lawyers in Nigeria did, and yet he has been deprived of his liberty; he has been thrown out of his job at the university; and he has been denied visits from his family and friends.

Clearly, only a person possessed of a death-wish would openly send President-for-Life Dr Hastings Kamuzu Banda a catalogue of his crimes against the people of Malawi. The otherwise perfectly sane Malawian 'dissident' is faced with only two options: to remain silent, or to leave town. This isn't a real choice in the sense that it can't be said to constitute an act of free will on the part of those who are forced into the position of having to make it; on the contrary, such a choice would never arise in a country which upheld the rule of law in the first place.

Faced with a country like Malawi, one's sense of hopelessness is quickly dispelled by the knowledge that tyranny thrives on the mystique of power, on the suspicion that authority is infinite –

like God, perhaps – and that to challenge it is futile. We are too small, too powerless; there is nothing we can do except submit to its dictates. But we have moved a long way from a world in which kings were invested with divine authority; which is why Fela Anikulapo-Kuti, the Nigerian musician, declared recently: 'Human rights na my property, you can't dash me my property.' Fela was only declaiming a fact of our world: that the individual's right to freedom is not even a matter for discussion. The onus is firmly placed at the feet of those who would deprive others of their liberty, not on those who have been silenced for speaking the truth.

But Fela was able to say what he did because, from the perspective of Jack Mapanje, he enjoys a relative freedom. It is for this reason that we who are able to do something, however small, however apparently innocuous, have an added responsibility towards those whose utterances, even in the privacy of a university bar, are *absolutely* circumscribed by an octogenarian neurotic. In the particular case of Jack Mapanje, we published details of his arrest and detention, alongside a selection of his banned poetry, at the same time as we informed other concerned organisations of his plight.

The response to the publicity we generated was touching. I remember especially the group of distinguished British writers who gathered outside the Malawi High Commission in London to read a selection of Mapanje's poetry. The fact that Mapanje wasn't released as a result of this and other protests doesn't in any way detract from the necessity of acting; and it occurred to me how much more likely his release might have been if the demonstration of solidarity by those British writers had been repeated simultaneously in Lagos and Dakar; in those African capitals where intellectuals – and not only intellectuals – are still able to exercise their right to congregate in public.

It's not merely that this was a clear enough instance of an African writer illegally detained in an African prison *because he was a writer*, and that the African voice, raised in condemnation of an African crime, would have lent an undeniable moral authority to the world-wide disgust at the outrage being perpetrated. It's not even that if we really mean to challenge the historical imbalance between Africa and Europe, an imbalance which dictates, amongst other things, that the magazine I work for is located in London, then we cannot allow the European world to continue to exercise a monopoly on those moral values, which is what happens when it is they who are seen to take the initiative on issues which directly concern us. But more pertinent than either of these considerations is that if we want to rid our continent of the tyrannical regimes which seem bent on laying it to waste, then we are obliged to confront these regimes on the basis of their illegitimacy. Hastings Banda, Daniel arap Moi, Master Sergeant Samuel Doe: these are the perversions of Africa, not its representatives. And every time one of them imprisons a poet, let's make sure that we shout as loudly and as clearly as possible.

Africa must monitor Africa. This is the pre-requisite for mastering the reality which will otherwise continue to have us at its mercy. Those Nigerian lawyers understood this only too well, which was why they then proceeded to act in ways that might seem foolhardy to those who possess no higher notion of the continent's destiny than that which is displayed by the above-named lunatics. The courage and the vision displayed by those CLO lawyers provide at least one source of hope at a time when, after three decades of independence, one sees any amount of evidence that our continent is on the point of collapse. The challenge that we now face is to extend what they have begun. In any case, I don't see that we have any choice in the matter. If we don't seize the time – and the opportunity offered by this conference – then it will be too late for all of us.

*Paper addressed to a conference on 'The Writer and Human Rights,' held in Dakar, Senegal, in September 1989.

97

Waste and rumours of waste

The sight of Kenya's President, Daniel arap Moi, making the right environmental noises at the recent conference in London was only less ridiculous than the image of Mrs Thatcher, the conference organiser, putting herself forward as the world's leading statesperson on all matters green. Toxic waste dumping in Africa is, after all, the prime example of market forces in operation: industrial by-products of the wealthy nations on the one hand; bankrupt African nations with plenty of land on the other. The temptation is irresistible, hence the proliferation of international cowboys operating out of bogus London offices. One hardly needs a degree in economics to grasp the principles involved, which are just as horrific as those which underpinned the Atlantic Slave Trade. The pity of it is that corrupt African officials have once again undervalued their available resources: two dollars and fifty cents per ton of waste delivered to Benin according to the terms of a secret contract dated 12 January 1988, against a possible figure of three thousand dollars per ton.

Still, Kenya has not yet figured on the list of those African countries threatened with death by slow poison, but perhaps this has been an oversight on the part of those people who are prepared to make money out of murder: 'If anything happens to the Africans because of the waste, that's too bad,' was the chilling formulation of one such merchant. But there's at least an even chance that the censorship of alternative voices in Kenya has extended beyond the narrowly political, a stricture which immediately leads one to contemplate a more elastic definition of just what constitutes an environmental hazard, at least as far as the imprisoned dissidents are concerned. More than one exiled Kenyan opposition group recently claimed that the United States army had been granted permission by the authorities to conduct drug-related medical experiments on a rural community in the north-east of the country. If this rumour is false then the Kenyan government is free to tell us so, at length if necessary, but we already know that they will do no such thing. A previous article in *Index on Censorship* which detailed allegations of torture in that country's prisons failed to elicit even a denial from the High Commission in London.

As in Kenya, so elsewhere: the continent is weighed down by authoritarian regimes whose grip on the machinery of the State is directly related to the amount of foreign exchange they are able to spend on the sophisticated military hardware – communist or otherwise – which maintains them in power. When you consider that there isn't a single African country threatened with foreign invasion – the front-line States excepted – you also have to consider the phenomenon of the national army as a deliberate instrument of internal control. And so it happens: in Benin, for instance, where over two hundred people are currently believed to be held in detention for their opposition to the twenty-year rule of President Matthieu Kerekou (in God's name, go!), troops were recently ordered to shoot protesting civil servants demanding seven months' salary arrears. This is to say nothing about the perks which are consequent on power, including German motor cars and English boarding schools. One may as well ask why tyrants are so predictable as wonder why the ordinary Beninois, observing the cavalcade of Wa-Benzi* from a perspective roughly equivalent to that of the gutter, don't simply tear down the entire structure. According to yet another rumour (so many rumours!), the attempt to do just this in the north-east of Kenya in 1982 led to the slaughter of one thousand five hundred peasants by members of the security forces.

Kerekou's government is desperate for foreign exchange, but

so are the governments of Angola and Gabon and the Congo and Liberia and Sierra Leone and Equatorial Guinea and Mauretania, all of which are also suspected of secret deals for the disposal of toxic waste. By the nature of the case these rumours are impossible to verify; but what else is one to believe when the same merchant who was ready to dispose of any number of human beings (but only Africans), also claims to have bribed a number of Liberian officials in order to secure the five hundred-acre site in the interior on which he hopes to make his fortune? Those with even limited experience of African officials know that this is a simple matter. The continent is at the mercy of the American dollar, which means that anything goes. And if the Liberian authorities themselves take such a casual attitude towards the security and well-being of their own citizens, why should a foreign merchant be criticised for the same? One hundred, one thousand, one million: what does it matter when we already know that Africans have too many children anyway? Toxic waste as population control – a pleasing symmetry – would neatly dispose of two problems, without even the necessity for government intervention. This last would meet with the approval of the IMF, to say nothing of the World Bank, which never tires of criticising expensive welfare programmes.

Examples of private enterprise already abound: last November, the Portuguese press reported negotiations between the Angolan government and a Swiss arms dealer to import five million tons of industrial waste in exchange for two million dollars and the construction of a new city, port and airfield; a European consortium recently announced plans to set up an incinerator for 'household refuse' near Freetown, the capital of Sierra Leone, to generate electricity for local use. There's no doubt that the inhabitants of Freetown are in urgent need of electricity, which is currently rationed to a few hours each day, but the discovery of a toxic waste dump on the outskirts of the city last August will hardly convince them that the term 'household rubbish' isn't just a euphemism for more deadly cargo. The government, of course, has been making all the appropriate noises about monitoring this rubbish, but they can hardly be expected to do otherwise. In any case, the Sierra Leone government is notoriously inept – a consequence of corruption – which is why it would be foolhardy to imagine that they were capable of distinguishing mercury-laced sludge from used tea bags.

This is the most frightening aspect of the toxic waste scandal in Africa: not merely that one is forced to disbelieve everything one is told by the interested parties; but, further, that one is obliged to believe in rumours. And in so far as the Kenyan High Commission in London ignores our scurrilous articles they are right in this respect at least: that we wouldn't believe whatever they said to the contrary.

*Swahili for 'owners of Mercedes Benz'.

Suffer the little children

There were riots in Lusaka the month before I arrived. The IMF had forced the government to remove the subsidy on mealie-meal, in effect doubling the price of the nation's staple food, and the city had erupted. The most serious disturbances occurred on the university campus, but only after the para-military had been despatched to crack a few skulls. 'When they send in those guys you must know that the time for compromise is over,' was the way that Daniel, my journalist friend, put it. Now the university was closed, but the evidence of the brutality inflicted by the armed wing of the ruling United National Independence Party (UNIP) was everywhere to be seen in the broken doors and smashed windows.

This was the first time in twenty-six years of independence that such a thing had happened in Zambia, and President Kenneth Kaunda was sufficiently shaken to agree to a hasty referendum on multi-party democracy. A date was set and disaffected ex-UNIP politicians crawled out of obscurity only to be shoved back again when the continent's elder statesman had recovered from his initial trauma. It seemed that he had been precipitate; October was much too soon. 'The people' (or 'the masses', I forget which) wouldn't be ready to take such a momentous decision concerning the country's political future until August next year – at the earliest. And now everybody was in doubt as to how far, precisely, they were even permitted to discuss the issue, at least in public.

That was why, presumably, General Tembo (retired), the most likely of the presidential hopefuls, refused to declare in favour of democracy at the press briefing he called, even though he insisted that he intended to put himself at the disposal of the most 'progressive forces' in the country. What did he mean by progressive? He didn't want to say at this early stage but, well . . . progressive. One began to wonder, in fact, why he had bothered to call the briefing at all, until somebody pointed out that the whole of Zambia didn't contain half the number of journalists who were supposed to be gathered in that room, and that Tembo, who had only recently been released after two years in prison, could yet find himself incarcerated again on charges of treason.

In short, nobody quite knew what was happening, including, it soon transpired, the father of the nation himself. He, too, gathered the press together, but then insisted on answering all the questions, from the economy to his possible successor, with reference to the Scriptures. This in itself wasn't unusual. Everybody knows the mission-educated son of a preacher to be a deeply religious man ('religious faith has played a central role in my life'), hence his 'philosophy' of Humanism, the country's official ideology since 1967.

Finding a clear-cut definition of Humanism is difficult indeed, largely because Kaunda's own pronouncements on the subject are vague and often contradictory. However, in *Letter to my Children*, one of his numerous publications, he himself describes it as a kind of Christianised Marxism which 'operates on the boundary between religion and politics as a channel for the best gifts of all true faith: compassion, service, and love – to be lavished on the nation's people.'

Letter to my Children is an interesting document, less for its politics (confused), than for what it tells us about the man (more confused). He himself offers it as an explanation of 'what makes me tick – my philosophy, if you like; the things I believe and why I believe them', but not in the way he imagines; for instance:

Africans are born, I think, with an innate sense of rhythm – the beat of drums sends pulses through our systems and awakens deep emotions and strange feelings that link us to our ancestors from time immemorial.

Again:

The coming of Christianity had a complex effect on (the) African world view, partly disrupting and partly enlarging it. I don't want to get bogged down in all that business though. It is enough to say that I feel within myself the tension created by the collision of these two world views which I have never completely reconciled. It is a ludicrous and indeed insulting over-simplification to claim, as some missionaries have done, that we non-Western peoples are still deepdown pagan with a top dressing of Christianity.

One has to remind oneself, when reading this book, that the writer is a Head of State, responsible for the well-being of almost eight million people. Out of respect, therefore, we might be inclined to pass over in silence the implications of the first passage, only to be confronted by the very same problem in the second: that of a man with a fragile notion of his own identity, never mind the collective identity of the people over whom he is pleased to rule.

'I'm haunted', he tells us, 'by the fear that the massive power the nation has entrusted to me may . . . violate the integrity of those who are on the receiving end of such power.' But language has betrayed him. The 'massive power' to which he refers* was seized, not given, and in the very year, 1973, that he wrote these words. In any case, the condition of powerlessness is, by definition, a violation of integrity, which is why power is always taken, never freely given; but the fact that Kaunda imagines he can delude 'those who are on the receiving end' as easily as he can delude himself tells us what he thinks of them as surely as it explains the title of his book.

In this Kaunda is typical enough. All African leaders despise their subjects (never citizens), which is why they behave in the ways they do towards them. The only difference is one of style. Unlike his neighbour, President-for-Life Dr Hastings Kamuzu Banda ('The Malawi system, the Malawi style is that Kamuzu says it's that, and then it's finished. Whether anyone likes it or not, that is how it's going to be here')†, Kaunda professes a more circumspect – or more hypocritical – approach, one that permits him to talk about 'the right to active participation in the political life, to a measure of consent in the form of government, *to free association and free debate*' (my italics), while he turns Zambia into a one-party state and imprisons his political opponents.

Banda doesn't give a damn what his people think of him; Kaunda wants his children to reciprocate the 'compassion, service, and love' that he lavishes on them; hence:

> Every wise parent learns that though he has the physical strength to compel his children to obey him . . . he must refrain from using such power in the belief that patient example is a better teacher than the whip. The parent-child relationship is one common example of the truth that the test of mastery of power is the willingness to refrain from using it. It may sound paradoxical, but experience has taught me that such a gamble can pay off.

But now his children were rebelling, and the Great African Chief, pagan or not but with flywhisk (or – modern times – handkerchief) in hand, was stunned. And since it wasn't possible for him to imagine that he had actually been rejected by his children, he told himself instead that democracy was the name of the game.

However: 'We can't cope with democracy. This isn't the West. We're still too backward.' The speaker was a moderately successful businessman in his early forties. I say moderately: he was on his way to Johannesburg to buy a secondhand car – 'a Mercedes, or perhaps a BMW, what do you think?' – before flying to South Korea and Taiwan to seal a couple of deals. This made him positively wealthy in a country where the average monthly wage was less than the new price of a bag of mealie-meal, and where owning a car, no matter its condition, was generally taken as a sign of prosperity.

The taxi driver I spoke to the following day concurred.

'Do you like politics?' I asked, picking up his newspaper and glancing at the latest agency reports on the civil war in Liberia.

'Too much,' he said.

'What do you think of this multi-party business?'

'It's not good,' he said without hesitation. 'Just watch, when these politicians start their nonsense we're going to have trouble in this country. Better leave it as it is. One party is good for us.'

Later, when I got back to Daniel's place, I asked him what he thought of all this. He simply shrugged and wouldn't be drawn. For a journalist, he was a man of few opinions. In fact all he wanted to talk about for the fortnight that I stayed with him was his impending trip to a college in the north of England, where he had been accepted on a one-year journalism course. He was now busy trying to raise the money. A local businessman had offered to help by providing the kwacha equivalent of Daniel's foreign exchange allocation; the businessman, in return, would take half the sterling – £5,000 – at the official rate, which was less than half the black market rate. But the balance would only cover Daniel's fees; he still had to find the money for board and lodging.

With all this to think about, he had little time for the multi-party debate, or so I mistakenly – and charitably – assumed. And I could see very well that food was a more pressing problem. He earned three thousand kwacha a month – £25 – after deduction for the rent on his bungalow. On the day I met him, for instance, he was preparing to eat his first meal in twelve hours, a bowl of mealie-meal made into a kind of porridge. I insisted that we go to the nearby market, where I filled his shopping bag with every-thing in sight. He was shocked at my extravagance. He thought six hundred kwacha (£5) was a lot of money, and in his terms it was.

But however poor, he still recognised that he was more fortunate that his married colleages: 'If you go into their houses you will be shocked. Some of these senior editors don't even have a bed to sleep on.' Daniel himself had a bed but little else: he owned just two shirts (both frayed at the collar), two pairs of trousers (one too short and the other too big around the waist), and one pair of leather shoes (but without the heels).

He did volunteer, once, that Kaunda should have stepped down last year, when he was still quite popular, but that the people hated him now and might even kill him if he attempted to retire. But that was all he would say. Besides, what did his opinions matter? He couldn't publish them; he couldn't even publish the relatively mild criticisms in the 'letters to the editor' which arrived on his desk at the rate of two or three a week. So he concentrated on his trip to England instead, and roped me in to help. It seemed that the businessman was beginning to have doubts about the scheme. Mightn't Daniel disappear with the money once he was abroad? Wouldn't it be safer, if more expensive, to buy his sterling on the black market? And now he was prevaricating over the letter to the bank manager which stood between Daniel and Darlington.

'If he sees you he'll be shamed into keeping his word,' Daniel said. I was sceptical, but I should have known better. This was his country, after all. In the event, we were kept waiting only half an hour. 'You saw how uncomfortable you made him? I knew it; I knew he wouldn't be able to give me any excuses.' Darlington had moved that much closer, and now he wanted me to tell him more about England. 'So it's cold up there, eh?' he said, and pretended to shiver; but even on a windy, mid-winter morning in Zambia he couldn't conceive of real cold. England itself was just a few photos of Darlington in the flashy prospectus, and the cultured, disembodied voices of the World Service announcers that we listened to every evening.

The BBC, in fact, was his only source of information about the outside world, including events in his own continent. It happened, for instance, that there were new developments in the Liberian civil war, with the neighbouring countries about to despatch a peace-keeping force to stop the carnage. Such direct intervention in the internal affairs of another African country was a momentous development, but any hope (always hope) that Nigeria was about to assert its position as the regional heavy-weight was being undermined (again) by the country's familiar anxiety not to be seen to be pushing its weight around.

But even here Daniel didn't seem terribly interested; and while he might have argued that the possible repercussions of the Liberian conflict for the future of Zambia were sufficiently remote for him to safely ignore, the unexpected developments in the Middle East – the Iraqi invasion and subsequent annexation of Kuwait – were of a different order altogether. Iraq was Zambia's sole supplier of crude oil, which Iraq sold at a reduced rate in return for copper, Zambia's sole (and rapidly diminishing) foreign exchange earner. Zambia simply didn't possess the necessary reserves of hard currency to buy oil on the open market. Sure enough, within forty-eight hours there were five-mile queues outside the petrol stations, and this was only the beginning. Another week and whatever industry the country possessed – little enough, God knows – would be forced to shut down.

I've said that Daniel couldn't afford the luxury of political opinions, even where they concerned his own country, but this wasn't the whole story. In fact Daniel, along with the business-man and the taxi-driver, exhibited a base level of political consciousness that chimed perfectly with the President's own sentiments. If Kaunda thought of his people as children to be led by the guiding hand of the all-wise, all-powerful father ('Every wise parent learns that though he has the physical strength to compel his children to obey him . . .'), they themselves re-sponded in suitably infantile fashion. And if Kaunda was now hated; if his people wanted him to go, it wasn't because they had matured politically overnight and suddenly discovered the virtues of democracy, but because their father was seen to have failed them. He couldn't deliver; he couldn't even guarantee the price of a bag of mealie-meal. He was revealed as human, after all, and the people rioted. The only option left to him was to exploit whatever physical strength he still possessed in order to maintain himself in power, which was why he didn't hesitate to despatch the para-military against protesting students when even he recognised that the reciprocal love he expected from his people was unable to transcend the simple fact of hunger.

August 1990

*The President of the Republic of Zambia is Head of State and Commander-in-Chief of the Armed Forces. Presidential powers include the appointment of a Prime Minister, a Secretary-General of the Party, an Attorney-General, a Director of Public Prosecutions, a Chief Justice and judges of the Supreme Court.
†From a speech by Banda to the Legislative Assembly